New SAT Essay Prep

**24 Actual Sample Essays with
Detailed and Logical Problem Analyses**

New SAT Essay Prep

**24 Actual Sample Essays with
Detailed and Logical Problem Analyses**

CONTENTS

What is the difference between content analysis and rhetorical analysis?

The difference, as a matter of fact, is rather simple. The content analysis is to discuss if you, as a critic, agree or disagree with the author's point of view, or central idea. Sometimes, you can talk about why you don't agree with the author's minor argument(s) while you don't have any problems with the author's main argument, or the central idea, or the thesis statement. Thus, the content analysis is basically concerned with WHAT the author is talking about. On the other hand, the rhetorical analysis is all about HOW the author is talking about the central idea, or HOW the author is conveying this central idea. Therefore, in any rhetorical analysis, you are not supposed to say anything about your argument on WHAT the author is talking about. Never.

What then is a rhetorical analysis? As mentioned above, a rhetorical analysis is about HOW the author is conveying his or her central idea, and normally, there are 3 different ways of doing this. These are called rhetorical devices. Three typical rhetorical devices are as follows.

1. Examples
2. Style
3. Reasoning

1. Examples

Giving examples is the most typical way of providing evidence, so giving an example is essentially the same thing as providing evidence. There are a few types of examples; scientific, authoritative, statistical, and personal examples. In practice, scientific and authoritative examples can be the same thing, just as scientific examples can be the same as statistical examples and authoritative examples the same as statistical examples. However, personal examples are quite different from any of the other type of examples.

2. Style

There are too many stylistic elements to cover completely in this introductory manual, but the following are among the most important:

(A) Literary devices including Irony, Sarcasm, Paradox, Rhetorical Questions
(B) Strong diction
(C) Appealing to emotion

(A) Literary devices including Irony, Sarcasm, Paradox, Rhetorical Question

Discussing a literary device is never an easy task in any context, but it must be done if the author uses one because, if properly used, a literary device is a very powerful tool to convey any argument. The focus here is on identifying them as the primary or outstanding rhetorical device used in the passage. Exactly how to do this will be explained in detail later in this manual.

(B) Strong diction

One of the biggest problems encountered when discussing strong diction is that individual students understand diction in a very subjective manner; if a certain word seems a bit unfamiliar, students are likely to think that the word in question is a difficult one and that the author is therefore using strong diction. When this happens in class, I cannot avoid being frustrated. So what is the best way to identify strong diction? This will be explained in great detail later in this manual.

(C) Appealing to emotion

When appealing to our emotions, an author also uses a literary device, so we must be very careful with our analysis.

3. Reasoning

Even though there are an unlimited number of reasoning devices, the passages or essays you may be asked to analyze will contain a very limited set of these. Providing a more complete set would make it extremely difficult for ETS to evaluate your analyses and that would be too time-consuming and therefore impractical.

The most popular reasoning devices are Cause & Effect and Comparison & Contrast. The possibility that you will encounter other reasoning devices on one of these tests is practically none, so there is no need to waste time preparing for them.

What must be included in Rhetorical Analysis

1. As explained above, the examples, style, and reasoning devices used by the author must be included in your analysis. However, it is not necessary to include *all* these three elements or devices in your analysis. Just the most outstanding elements need to be included in your discussion; two is usually more than enough. In fact, it is not advisable to deal with all three elements, because doing so tends to make your analysis seem digressive and/or disorganized. Additionally, you wouldn't have that kind of time. So, with this in mind, we will limit our focus to just two elements, any two of those mentioned above: examples, styles, and reasoning devices.

2. Thus, a combination of any two elements must be included in your analysis unless there is only ONE outstanding element, which is very unlikely because ETS does not use such passages for grading purposes.

3. However, this only refers to your introduction; in your main body, you must specify what you have identified in the introduction. Examples.are as follows.

(A) Cause & Effect

This is a typical reasoning device. If you give Cause & Effect as an outstanding element in your introduction, you must clearly identify what the cause is and what effect is in the main body, and these examples of Cause & Effect must be taken directly from the passage being analyzed.

(B) Comparison & Contrast

This is a typical reasoning device. If you give Comparison & Contrast as an outstanding element in your introduction, you must clearly state what the comparison is and what the contrast is in the main body, and these examples of Comparison & Contrast must be taken directly from the passage being analyzed.

(C) Literary techniques including Irony, Sarcasm, and Rhetorical Questions

These are typical stylistic elements. If you give one or more literary techniques as outstanding element in your introduction, you must clearly state what these literary techniques are in the main body, and the examples of these literary techniques must be taken directly from the passage being analyzed.

(D) Strong diction

This is a typical stylistic element. If you identify strong diction as an outstanding element in your introduction, you must clearly state what that strong diction is in the main body, and these examples of strong diction must be taken directly from the passage being analyzed.

(E) Diverse examples

This is a typical way of providing evidence. If you give diverse examples as an outstanding element in your introduction, you must clearly state what these diverse examples are in the main body, and these examples of diverse examples must be taken directly from the passage being analyzed.

When writing the main body and expanding upon the author's devices you have identified in your introduction, you must be cautious of the following.

1. Diverse Examples are not simply various examples. There are differences between Diverse Examples and their various counterparts. What you need to identify is a Diversity of examples not a variety of them. Diverse Examples will typically be Statistical, Scientific, Authoritative, or Personal examples. Of course, Diversity can be understood as a sort of variety, but for practical purposes, we will ignore this particular way of looking at Diversity and variety. If you find examples of these in the passage you are analyzing, you must identify them using the words "Diverse" or "Diversity" and avoid using the words "various" or "variety".

2. In order for you to identify the author's diction as strong diction, you must prove why it is strong. There are two ways to do this.

(A) Synonyms

In order to argue that the author has used strong diction, you can provide an alternative weaker synonym that the author did not use. For example, if the author used the word "despicable", instead of "bad", you can argue that this is strong diction because "despicable" conveys a stronger feeling and that the author is trying to express a sense of decaying morality. However, to do this effectively, you must state the alternative synonym "bad" to make sure that the ETS evaluator understands that you know what you are talking about. However, be aware that, unless you can provide very clear examples to back up your argument, discussing strong diction can be rather tricky.

(B) Combining strong diction with stylistic elements

This is a common and effective combination. Thus, discussing strong diction with stylistic elements is very effective, such as with Irony, Sarcasm, Simile and Rhetorical Question. A possible example is as follows.

"Selling those products to kids of any ages is like selling a destroyed future to the young generation"; the literary technique used here is simile and "destroyed future" is an example of strong diction. The expression, "destroyed future" is by itself nothing special. Nor can it be regarded as strong diction by itself, but because it is used with "selling", it has become more powerful and effective than saying "their future is destroyed" because you should not sell anything that has been "destroyed".

This way of showing strong diction is more productive and easier than utilizing synonyms, so remember that discussing strong diction in combination with any literary technique is very effective. Of course, this is true only when the author combines the two. Fortunately good authors tend to do this.

 **SUMMARY AT THIS POINT**

1. What must be included in the introduction:

(A) Identification of the author's outstanding rhetorical devices

(B) TWO of those devices are enough

(C) Words that must be stated, not implied: Diverse Example, Strong Diction, Diversity, Irony, Sarcasm, Simile, Rhetorical Questions, Cause & Effect, and Comparison & Contrast

2. What must be included in the main body:

(A) Specification of those devices identified in the introduction

(B) These must be based on specific example(s) taken directly from the passage being analyzed

Please try to master this strategy before we go on to assessing each individual essay and determining how to properly apply this strategy to the sample essays.

Getting a very good score vs. getting the perfect score

If you have closely followed all the instructions so far, you can get a score of 20 or 22 out of 24, which is a very good score. However, even when following all the instructions, getting a perfect score of 24 is not that easy for most students.

Why it is so hard to get the perfect score

It is not easy to show why the author's rhetorical devices are effective in conveying the central idea. In order to better understand this, let's review what must be done to get 20-22.

1. Identification of the author's rhetorical devices in the introduction
2. Specification of the author's devices identified in the introduction.
3. Explanation of why those devices are effective in conveying the central idea.

1 and 2 are much easier than 3, because 3 depends solely on what the central idea is, and there is no way you can be prepared for all the possible central ideas. However, as explained above in this manual, 1 and 2 can be generalized regardless of the central idea. You can always resort to pretending that you explained why the author's rhetorical devices are effective in conveying the central idea. The trick is very simple; stating some reason should be enough, even if the reason doesn't make much sense. ETS evaluators are usually in a hurry and do not have enough time to read and carefully assess each individual essay. Here is an example;

The author's this kind of approach based on Comparison & Contrast is very powerful in conveying the central idea because without realizing the actual causes of the current environmental problems the general public will have poor understanding of the genuine impact of them.

Even if what is explained after "because" in this particular example is somewhat irrelevant to the central idea, whoever wrote this tried to explain why Comparison & Contrast is effective and that is usually good enough to get the student a score of 20-22, assuming he or she doesn't have other problems with the writing itself, such as errors in grammar. However, if the reasoning that comes after "because" is correct, the student could easily get a score of 24.

ACTUAL READINGS FOR THE ANALYSIS
AND SAMPLES OF CORRESPONDING ESSAYS

Reading 1
Adapted from David Bell,
"In defense of Drones: A Historical Argument,"
www.newrepublic.com, 1/27/2012.
＊(8-1 from summer classes of 2017)

Reading 2
Adapted from Anonymous, "The Virtue of Business:
How Markets Encourage Ethical Behavior,"
Institute for Faith, Work, and Economics
＊(8-2 from summer classes of 2017)

Reading 3
＊somehow, with no reference(9-1 from summer classes of 2017)
Argument over the relative contributions of practice
and native talent to the development of elite performance

Reading 4
＊somehow, with no reference(9-2 from summer classes of 2017)
Argument over security and privacy in data storage
and transfer, especially on the net

Reading 5
＊somehow, with no reference(10-1 from summer classes of 2017)
Argument over the possibility of animals feeling pain

Reading 6
Adapted from Lindsey Lusher and Benjamin Shute,
"Keep Farmland for Farmers,"
2013 by the New York Times Company.
Originally published September 20, 2013.
＊(10-2 from summer classes of 2017)

READING 1

N E W S A T
E S S A Y
P R E P
S A T
E S S A Y
P R E P
N E W S A T
E S S A Y
P R E P
S A T
E S S A Y
P R E P
N E W S A T
E S S A Y
P R E P
S A T
E S S A Y
P R E P
N E W S A T
E S S A Y
P R E P
S A T
E S S A Y
P R E P
N E W S A T
E S S A Y
P R E P

Sample Essay 1

Student Rainbow
예비12, 2017 계관웅어학원 SAT 700반

War has developed through the years where tactics, technology, weapons and many other features have been altered. Drone warfare has become one of the emerging methods incorporated in the American military. Although effective as it seems, David Bell argues that military use of drones does not eliminate restraints on carrying out deadly destruction of an enemy's land and people. He uses diverse exemplification such as authoritative and historical evidence, and strong rhetoric devices such as sarcasm.

Firstly, Bell cities historic and authoritative evidence to reveal the hidden unethical effects of drone. Firstly, he referred to the "law professor Mary Ellen o'connell," who argued that "killing far from battlefields where there is an understanding of necessity is ethically troubling." This authoritative evidence effectively backs up Bell's argument as Bell also points out that when enemies are not near and a mere "remote control" can cause a devastating effect, it can numb the humaness and ethics at the military. Similarly, Bell cities "The Economist," in which they asked if the risk to the life be gone in one side, then does "the vital form of restraint also disappear?" This idea that the military will cease to carry a moral and just perspective cautions the audience as war itself is already a immoral activity despite its seemingly moral goals. Bell also brings in historical evidence whereby he mentions that Germans in "1918" developed guns that allowed "anomity of railing." Also associating this with the notorious reputation of Germany, the readers grasp the sense of unjustness and ethical flaws of such tactics and weapons. Also, he brings an example from the 1500's where gunpowder weapons were thought as a "wicked and terrible discovery which had destroyed ⋯ the virtue to nought." Presented with variety of misterical and authoritative criticisms of long distance weapons, the readers are cautered to a significant moral issue that follows such weapons.

Next, Bell points out the benefits of drone warfare to emphasis the immorality of it. He acknowledges that drone warfare aims to safeguard American lives and also put a premium on other lives for very practical and political reasons. Although it seems very embracing towards the benefits of drones, the words "practical" and "political" along with his expression "putting a premium on other lives," create a strong atmosphere of sarcasm to the audience. This sarcasm helps the audience to belittle the positive side of drone warfare while inclining towards the negative side. Bell continues on to mention that opposing perspectives highlight the minimised damage of the American civilians. Although it seems quite compensating, the audience then realite it is merely for "political effects," but not for "moral outrage." Through using sarcasm, Bell effectively disputes the opposing critics.

Problem 1:

The first two sentences are spent on giving an opinion as to the central idea of the given reading. This is a problem because that is part of content analysis, but this is supposed to be a rhetorical analysis.

Problem 2:

Student Rainbow failed to identify one outstanding reasoning device that the author used: comparison and contrast. ETS evaluators do not have enough time to read and carefully assess each submitted essay. The general understanding is that they would have 10-20 minutes to do the job. Therefore, the introduction becomes relatively more important than when the evaluator has enough time, because the evaluator will have to decide how carefully to read the rest of essay based on what is in the introduction.

Problem 3:

The way the main body starts is very confusing because in it the student, a critic, is claiming that the author of the reading is criticizing the use of drone by saying "… reveal the hidden unethical effect of drones." In other words, it sounds as though this student didn't really understand the author's intention of talking about "the unethical effects of drones" because these quotes in the second and third paragraphs of the given reading are what the author of the given reading is planning on refuting later in the reading. However, according to the way the critique is written, it sounds as if the author of the reading is criticizing the use of drones, which is totally opposite of the author's intention. Something like this happens either because students tend to write in too much of a hurry, or because they are not thinking about what they are writing when they are writing it. This is a common mistake.

Problem 4:

Probably because this student had hard time understanding the author's true intention with the quotes as noted in Problem 3, he or she wrongly claims that in the second paragraph of the critique, "Bell points out the benefits of drone warfare to emphasis[emphasize] the immorality of it." But in fact Bell points out the benefits because he believes in them, not to stress the immorality. This happened because as commented in Problem 3, the student did not realize the way Bell is refuting the arguments of some critics to establish his own central idea.

Problem 5:

There are many serious grammatical errors; in the second paragraph of the critique "···variety of···" when the correct expression is 'a variety of,' and in the third paragraph "···to emphasis···" when correct grammar is 'to emphasize'; these are fundamental mistakes.

Never put down anything that's not the author's [red annotation]

NAME: Class:

write more legibly [red annotation]

War has developed through the years where tactics, technology, weapons and many other features have been altered. Drone warfare has become one of the ~~newly~~ emerging methods incorporated in the American military. Although ~~effective~~ as it seems, David Bell argues that military use of drones does not eliminate restraints on carrying out deadly destruction of an enemy's land and people. He uses diverse exemplification such as authoritative and historical evidence, ~~strong reasoning as cause and effect and its refutation~~ and strong rhetoric devices such as sarcasm.

    Firstly, Bell ~~cites~~ cites historic and authoritative evidence to reveal the hidden ~~unethicality~~ • unethical effects of drone. Firstly, he referred to ~~a~~ the "law professor Mary Ellen O'connell," who argued that "killing far from battlefields where there is an understanding of necessity is ethically ~~troubling~~." This authoritative evidence ~~effectively backs up~~ Bell's argument as Bell also ~~states~~ points out that when enemies are not near ~~or troops are not~~ and a mere ~~click can~~ "remote control" can cause a devastating effect, it can numb the humaness and ~~ethica~~ ethics of the military. Similarly, Bell cites "The Economist," in which they asked if the risk to the life begone in one side, then ~~does~~ "the ~~restraint~~ vital form of restraint also disappear?" This idea that the military will cease to ~~bear the~~ carry a moral and just perspective ~~be~~ cautions the audience as war itself is (already) a immoral activity despite its seemingly moral goals. Bell also brings in historical

so what's the point? [red annotation]

evidence ~~when~~ he ~~mentions~~ mentions that Germans in ~~the~~ "1918" "developed guns" that allowed "enormity of killing." ~~Also~~ ~~relating~~ *associating this with* to the notorious reputation of Germany, the readers ~~grasp~~ *might gain will* the sense of unjustness and ethical flaws of such tactics and ~~other~~ weapons. Also, he brings an ~~next~~ example from the 1500's where gunpowder weapons where ~~thought th~~ as a "wicked and terrible discovery which had destroyed... [the virtue to mankind."

thought of as [red annotation]

Presented with ~~a~~ variety of historical and authoritative criticisms of long distance weapons, the readers are ~~cautioned~~ to an ~~moral~~ issue that follows *significant* such weapons.

sounds inconsistant [red annotation]   ? [red annotation]

    Next, Bell points out ~~that there are~~ *the* (benefits) of drone warfare to emphasis the

emphasize [red annotation]

immorality ~~of~~ it. He acknowledges that "drone warfare aims to safeguard American lives and also put a premium on other lives for very practical and political reasons. Although it seems ~~like~~ very ~~inclining~~ *embracing* towards the benefits of drones, the words "practical" and "political" ~~along with~~ with his ~~word~~ expression "putting a premium on other lives," create a strong atmosphere of ~~sarcasm~~ (+) the audience. This sarcasm helps the audience to

How do you know? [red annotation]

belittle the positive side of drone ~~warfare~~ while inclining towards the ~~negative~~ side. Bell continues on to mention that opposing perspectives highlight the minimized damage of the American ~~cil~~ civilians. Although it seems quite compensating, the ~~readers~~ audience then realize it is ~~merely~~ for "political effects," but not for "moral outrage."

??? [red annotation]

compassion & unfeel!! [red annotation, right margin]

Through using ~~sarcasm~~ sarcasm, Bell effectively ~~contest~~ disputes the opposing critics.
~~and the~~

1. You put down your own opinion regarding
    the central idea → You aren't supposed to do that
2. You missed one critical device ~~that~~
    the author used
3. a significant number of grammar
    mistakes
4. occasional cases of conjecture

$$3/2/3 = 8 \times 2 = 16/2\rlap{/}x$$

Sample Essay 2

Student Blue Moon
예비11, 2017 계관웅어학원 SAT 700반

Throughout the extract, David Bell builds an argument to persuade his audience that even the abolition of drones for military use would not stop the deadly destruction of an enemy's land and people. To support his claim Bell employs comparison and contrast, powerful diction, and authoritative example.

Firstly, Bell makes use of comparison and contrast to claim that modern technology weapons do not differ from the original weapons. By comparing bow and arrow to gunpowder weapons, he asserts that those two weapons are similar in that they add the anonymity by allowing them to kill enemies in distance. This supports his argument that advanced military technology should not be criticized as it is a modernation of old weapons used from the beginning of the warfare, leading to think that the use of drones for military use would not stop the deadly destruction.

Then, the author employs powerful diction to add power to expressed ideas. Throughout the passage, Campbell continuously criticizes beliefs or people by using sarcasm. In the third paragraph, Bell cricizes Ariosto, an Italian poet in the 1500s, for what he said. He did not directly criticized the poet, yet by following his argument that remote control warfare are same as bow and arrow with Ariosto's argument that 'wicked and terrible discovery destroyed martial glory and reduced valor and virtue to naught', he criticized not only Ariosto, but everyone who holds the same view. This is a very effective device which allows the readers to feel criticized, leading them to change their mind to not be the next target of the criticism.

Lastly, Bell gives a quote from a person in high social status to support his claim. He cites Notre Dame law professor Mary Ellen O'Connell who holds the same opinion on this matter. This is a very effective device which adds power, as professor gives an image of a person who had done numerous research, therefore giving more credibility to Bell's argument.

To conclude, Bell used authoritative example, sarcasm, and comparison and contrast to persuade the audience.

Problem 1:

One thing is very clear in this student's introduction. Student Rainbow of the Sample Essay 1 missed Cause & Effect, and student Blue Moon also missed it. The important point is clear and simple; many, if not all, students focus on one single reasoning device. In other words, if they manage to identify one reasoning device, they ignore all other reasoning devices. Instead of looking for a second reasoning device, they look for non-reasoning devices such as stylistic elements and/or evidence. But this is a very near-sighted approach because many authors use various types of reasoning devices in a single writing, especially when their central idea is subjective in nature, which true of many given readings in essay questions on SAT. So be very careful about this.

Problem 2:

Student Blue Moon made a critical error by arguing that the quoted Norte Dame Law professor holds the same opinion as the author, when the professor was quoted as an example to be refuted by the author. Sometimes authors quote examples in order to disagree with them, and this student missed the point completely.

Problem 3:

Problem 1 & 2 are interrelated because providing an example to be refuted and an example to support the author's central idea is a form of Comparison and Contrast. In other words, student Blue Moon did not appreciate the effect or meaning of Comparison & Contrast when mentioning it in the introduction. In fact, the student misunderstood the given reading itself.

[margin note: excerpt?]

Throughout the (extract), David Bell builds an argument to persuade his audience that even the abolition of drones for military use would not stop the deadly destruction of an enemy's land and people. To support his claim Bell employs comparison and contrast, powerful diction, and authoritative example.

[margin notes: y'u need too prove this   ? , ?]

Firstly, Bell makes use of comparison and contrast to claim that modern technology weapons ~~does~~ do not differ from the original weapons. By comparing bow and arrow to *kinds of* gunpowder weapons, he asserts that those two weapons are similar in that they add the anonymity by allowing them to kill enemies in distance. This supports his argument that advanced military technology should not be criticized as it is a ~~modernation~~ *modernization* of old weapons used from the beginning of the warfare, leading to think that the use of drones for military use would not stop the deadly destruction. *Not a proper sentence*

Then, the author employs powerful diction to add power to expressed ideas. Throughout the passage, Campbell continuously criticizes beliefs or people by using (sarcasm). In the third paragraph, Bell cricizes Ariosto, an italian poet in the 1500s, for ~~the~~ what he said. He (did) not directly (criticized) the poet, yet *he* by following his argument that remote control warfare are the same as bow and arrow with Ariosto's argument that 'wicked and terrible discovery destroyed martial glory and reduced valor and virtue to nought', he criticized not only (Ariosto, but) everyone who holds the same view. This is a (very effective) device which allows the reader to feel criticized, leading them to change their mind to not be the next target of

[margin note: why?]

the criticism.

Lastly, Bell gives a quote from a person in high social status to support his claim. He cites Notre Dame law professor Mary Ellen O'connell who holds the same opinion on this matter. This is a very effective device which adds power, as professor gives an image of a person who had done numerous research, therefore giving more credibility to Bell's argument.

To conclude, Bell used authoritative example, sarcasm, and comparison and contrast to persuade the audience.

Even though you closely followed class instructions about the introduction
1. there are significant grammatical mistakes
2. quite a few arguments without any support

$$3/2\frac{5}{3} = 8.5 \times 2 = 17/\frac{}{24}$$

Sample Essay **3**

Student Humpback
예비12, 2017 계관웅어학원 SAT 700반

In this passage, David Bell persuades the audience that the military use of drones does not eliminate restraints on carrying out deadly destruction of an enemy's land and people. The author mainly does this through the use of logical progression, facts and examples, and other persuasive elements.

With tactical reasoning and appeal to logos, Bell persuades the audience that using drones for military purposes do not intensify the current existing level of destruction of an enemy's land. The author clearly defines his audience in this passage, mainly American citizens who believe that military drones in the U.S. Army play a role in making the armed forces more aggressive in battles with others nations. By stating that "the U.S. has largely fought against irregular, insurgent forces and terrorists, and actual combat has mostly taken place at much closer range than [⋯]", the author is invalidating the common misconception that critics of the drone have, which is that drones play a significant role in the U.S. Army. Bell demonstrates that the drones are not widely used enough in order for the critics to believe that they are the main source of conflict intensification.

The author employs facts and examples in order to substantiate his belief that viewpoints against the use of drones is irrational. He indicates "By 1918, the Germans had developed guns that could fire 200 pound shells a distance of 80 miles, over a trajectory that took them to an altitude of over 130,000 feet." By giving the audience specifications of the guns that were developed, Bell stresses how this was a significant military advance at the time of invention. He implies that even though the critics complained about this type of invention in the beginning, they totally accept it as a basic, necessary military equipment. He communicates to the audience that the critics' opposing view on military drones will be temporary, and that if the audience sees the guns as normal inventions, they should not have any prejudiced opinions only about drones.

Lastly, Bell uses other stylistic elements to persuade the audience. He refers to certain organizations and figures to introduce a controversial issue that he will elaborate on in order to engage the audience.

Problem 1:

Unfortunately, student Humpback did not identify any of the author's rhetorical devices. This is a big problem, because it means that there might be not much to read in the main body.

Problem 2:

As expected in Problem 1, exactly the same thing happened in the main body. "Tactical reasoning" doesn't mean anything, nor can it explain anything, because there are too many tactical reasoning devices. Almost every reasoning device is some form of tactical reasoning device. Thus, this kind of identification is in effect the same as no identification at all. Additionally, in the third paragraph of the essay, this student mentioned "facts and examples". It is obvious that student Humpback has a habit of making vague arguments: too broadly identifying the author's devices is as bad as not identifying anything. In other words, this student seems to be avoiding proper specification, which renders the entire essay too weak to be a rhetorical analysis.

Problem 3:

In the last paragraph student Humpback argues, "Bell uses other stylistic elements to persuade the audience. He refers to certain organizations and figures to ⋯." The student is saying that referring to something is a stylistic element, which is absurd. Referring to something or someone can never be a stylistic element.

Week 8-1 EW	NAME:	Class: 1700

In this passage, David Bell persuades the audience that the military use of drones does not eliminate restraints on carrying out deadly destruction of an enemy's land and people. The author mainly does this through the use of logical progression, facts and examples, and other persuasive elements. *Not specific enough*

    With tactical reasoning and appeal to logos, Bell persuades the audience that using drones for military purposes do not intensify the current/level of destruction of to an enemy's land. existing The author clearly defines his audience in this passage, mainly American citizens who believe that military drones in the U.S. Army play a role in making the armed forces more aggressive in battles with other nations. By stating that "the U.S. has largely fought against irregular, insurgent forces and terrorists, and actual combat has mostly taken place at much closer range than ɛ ɟ", the author is invalidating the common misconception that critics of the drone have, which is that drones are play a significant role in the U.S. Army. Bell demonstrates that the drones are not widely used enough in order for the critics to believe that they are the main source of conflict intensification. *What kind of?*

    The author employs facts and examples in order to substantiate his belief that/drones is irrational. He indicates "By 1918, the [viewpoints against the use of] Germans had developed guns that could fire 200 pound shells a distance of 80 miles, over a trajectory that took them to an altitude of over 130,000 feet." By giving the audience specifications of the guns that were developed, Bell stresses how this was a significant military advance at the time of invention. He implies that even though the critics complained about this type of invention in the beginning, they totally accept it as a basic, necessary military equipment. He communicates to the audience that the critics' opposing view on military drones will be temporary as time will, and that ~~it is~~ if the audience sees the guns as normal inventions, they should not have any prejudiced opinions about drones.

Lastly, Bell uses other only stylistic elements to persuade the audience. He refers to certain organizations and figures to introduce a controversial issue that he will elaborate on in order to engage the audience.

Sample Essay 4

Student Shangri-La
예비12, 2017 계관옹어학원 SAT 700반

In "In Defense of Drones: A Historical Argument", David Bell builds a convincing argument to persuade the audience that the use of aircraft drones in wars does not eliminate restraints upon war, and that the restraints are more a matter of politics. The author strengthens his logic and persuasiveness through the usage of strong comparison and contrast between present and the past, and between traditional methods and new, advanced technological methods.

David Bells outlines the history of advancements in warfare technology and compare them with the drone aircraft, underlining a significant point that using advanced technology in warfare is not a new concept. Using phrases such as "From the beginnings of warfare", "Once upon a time", and "Over the centuries", Bells lists the numerous technological tools that were used in the past: bow and arrow, gunpowder, and guns. By revealing to the audience that people have been inventing technological tools to "more efficiently" kill opponents from as late as the 1500's, the author efficiently argues that the use of drones in warfare is merely another technological advancement, hinting to the audience that technological advancements is an unavoidable, necessary step in warfare. By making a comparison between drone aircrafts and military tools used in the past, Bells effectively encourages the audience into believing that the using of drones is not as immoral and destructive as they think, and successfully adds support to his central idea that the restrains upon war is not really caused by drones, but by politicians.

Bells also makes a clear distinction between the traditional method and the new method to further support his central claim. From the beginning of the passage he writes, "American military might was symbolized by the heavy boots ⋯ stomping ashore to reestablish order ⋯ Today, it is symbolized by unmanned drone aircraft, controlled by thousand of miles away," providing accurate context to introduce his point. He then reveals the benefits of drone aircrafts building support to hiscentral idea: "to kill enemies with minimum risk to themselves ⋯ safeguard American lives." By adding that soldiers who fight on battlefields "run very great risks", Bells clearly makes a contrast between the methods of using drones and fighting on feet, effectively pointing out that bombing from a distance does not necessarily remove restraints. By comparing and contrasting the two methods, Bells lets the audience better understand that the difference between using the two methods is only a matter of efficiency in killing, not, a matter of eliminating restraints.

Throughout the passage, David Bell offers a convincing argument explaining that what some think about using drones in warfare is a misconception, and that it does not necessarily reduce or remove restraints upon warfare. By the effective utilization of comparison and contrast, he successfully persuades the readers to agree with his claim.

Problem 1:

Just like the students of previous essays, this student failed to identify one outstanding reasoning device that the author used: Cause & Effect. As explained before, the ETS evaluator doesn't have enough time to read and assess each submitted essay carefully. The general understanding is that they would have 10-20 minutes to do the job. Therefore, as explained before, the introduction becomes relatively more important than when the evaluator has enough time, because he or she will have to decide how carefully to read the rest of essay based on what is in the introduction. Moreover, this comparison and contrast doesn't have to be explained such detail in the introduction. All you have to do here is identify it.

Problem 2:

Although the introduction lacks an outstanding element, the main body starts relatively fine by explaining in significant detail how the author of the reading used comparison and contrast. However, because the Cause & Effect is missing from the introduction, this particular critique has lost a huge chunk of what it is supposed to analyze.

Good side:

Despite Problems 1 & 2, student Shangri-La's analysis of the given reading is well structured and even precise, derived from the analysis of the author's rhetorical devices based on Comparison & Contrast.

What could have been much better:

This would have been much better if the element of Cause & Effect had been identified in the introduction and had then been used in the analysis in the main body in combination with the element of Comparison & Contrast.

In "In Defense of Drones : A Historical Argument", David Bells builds an convincing argument to persuade the audience that the use of aircraft drones in wars ~~is appropriate, and that the~~ doesnot eliminate restraints upon war, and that the restraints ~~upon war~~ are more a matter of politics. ~~rather than~~ The author strengthens his logic and persuasiveness through the usage of strong comparison and contrast between present and the past, and between traditional methods and ~~new,~~ advanced technological methods.

→ any other devices?

~~David Bells~~ David Bells outlines the history of advancements in warfare technology, ~~comparing~~ and compare them with the ~~air~~ drone aircraft, ~~undertiming~~ underlining a significant point that ~~these the~~ ~~military tec~~ advancements in using advanced technology in warfare is ~~no so~~ not a new concept. ~~Through~~ Using phrases such as "from the beginnings of warfare", "Once upon a time", and " Over the centuries", Bells lists ~~different~~ the numerous ~~techno militar~~ technological tools that were used in the past : ~~Heavy boots "Boo~~ bow and arrow, gun powder, and guns. By revealing to the audience that ~~these~~ ~~"immoral" tools of killing~~ people have been inventing technological tools to "more efficiently" kill opponents, ~~the author even~~ from as late as the 1500's, the author efficiently argues that the use of drones in warfare is merely another technological advancement, ~~telling the~~ hinting to the audience that, ~~they cause of the "moral~~ ~~cause of the technology about worries about the moral~~ should not worry ~~because of the~~ about "immorality" of the drones, but ~~because about~~ ⟶ technological advancements ~~in warfare~~ ⓘs ⟨an a unavoidable, necessary step in warfare, ~~and that the~~ By ~~making a compar~~ making a comparison between ~~a remote contr~~ drone aircrafts and ~~some~~ military tools used in the past, Bells ~~successfully emphasizes that~~ ~~emphasizes his point~~ effectively encourages the audience into believing that the using of drones is not as immoral and destructive as ~~some~~ they ~~think~~ might think, and successfully adds support to his central idea that the restrains upon war is not really caused by drones, but by politicians.

Bells ~~makes and provides the audience with another compari and/or further~~ also makes a clear distinction between the ~~traditional~~ method and the new method to further support his central claim. From the beginning of the passage he ~~states~~ writes , " American military might was symbolized by the heavy boots ~~of~~ ... stomping ashore to reestablish order ... Today, it is symbolized by unmanned drone aircraft, controlled by thousand of miles away", providing accurate context to introduce his ~~to~~ point. ~~He By arguing that By revealing~~ He then reveals the ~~intention tas~~ benefits of ~~aircraft drone~~ drone aircrafts ~~to emphasizing that~~ building support to his central idea : " to kill enemies with minimum risk to themselves ... safeguard American lives". By ~~finally~~ adding that soldiers who fight on battlefields "run very great risks", Bells clearly makes a contrast between ~~using~~ the methods of using drones and fighting on feet, ~~emphasizing that~~ effectively pointing out that ~~us~~ bombing from a distant does not necessarily remove restraints. By comparing and contrasting the two methods, Bells lets the audience better understand that the difference between using the two methods is only a matter of "efficiency in killing, not a matter of eliminating restraints.

Throughout the passage, David Bell offers a convincing argument explaining that what the public some think about drone aircraft using drones in warfare is a a misconception, and that it does not necessarily reduce or remove restraints upon warfare. By the effective utilization of comparison and contrast, he successfully persuades the readers to agree with his claim.

Except for you failed to identify a couple of outstanding elements in the introduction, this is a fairly well written, quite organized analysis

$$4/3/4 = 11 \times 2 = 22/24$$

An Improved Version
of Sample Essay 4
for achieving the maximum score

In "In Defense of Drones: A Historical Argument", David Bell builds a convincing argument to persuade the reader that the use of aircraft drones in wars does not eliminate restraints upon war, and that the restraints are more of a political matter. The author strengthens his logic and persuasiveness by the use of strong Comparison & Contrast between the present and the past, and between traditional methods and new advanced technological methods, in combination with another reasoning device based on Cause & Effect.

David Bell outlines the history of advancements in warfare technology, and, by comparing them with modern-day drone aircraft, effectively emphasized that using advanced technology in warfare is not a new concept, in doing so uses phrases such as "from the beginnings of warfare", "once upon a time", and "over the centuries". Still in the logical line of Comparison & Contrast, Bell further lists the numerous technological devices that were used in the past: the bow and arrow, gunpowder, and guns. By revealing to the reader that people have been inventing technological tools to "more efficiently" kill opponents from as early as the 1500's, the author effectively argues that the use of drones in warfare is merely another technological advancement, hinting to the reader that technological advancements are probably an unavoidable, necessary step in the development of warfare. By further making a comparison between modern drone aircraft and military equipment used in the past, Bell strongly encourages the reader to believe that using drones is not as immoral and destructive as they might think, and successfully adds support to his central idea that the limitations upon war are not really caused by drones, but rather by politicians. This reasoning device of Cause & Effect works particularly well with the integral device of Comparison & Contrast, because using these two devices together makes the author's argument sound very analytical, and in turn convincing; after all, these two are the core elements of any analytical approach. Additionally, introducing a new and critical factor, the politician, into the overall argument helps engage the reader in the central idea, because political concerns are among the most common and powerful concerns in lives of so any people.

In order to further support his central claim, Bell also makes a clear distinction between the traditional method and the new method. This is another example of Comparison & Contrast. At the beginning of the passage he writes, "American military might was symbolized by the heavy boots ⋯ stomping ashore to reestablish order ⋯ Today, it is symbolized by unmanned drone aircraft, controlled by thousands of miles away," providing a credible context in which to expand upon his point. He then reveals the benefits of drone aircraft, building support for his central idea: "to kill enemies with minimum risk to themselves ⋯ safeguard American lives." By adding that soldiers who fight on battlefields "run very great risks", Bell makes a clear contrast between the methods of using drones and of fighting on foot, thus effectively pointing out that bombing from a distance does not necessarily remove restraints. By comparing and contrasting the two methods, Bell allows the reader better understand that the difference between using the two methods is only a matter of efficiency in killing, not a matter of totally eliminating restraints.

Throughout the passage, David Bell offers a convincing argument explaining that there are common misconceptions related to using drones in warfare and that using drones does not necessarily remove or even reduce restraints upon warfare. The author effectively utilizes comparison and contrast, and combines this with another reasoning device, Cause & Effect. This combination is a very powerful method of conveying the central idea which is important because this kind of central idea runs the risk of being considered very subjective, and therefore the author needs to use an ample amount of logical reasoning and take full advantage of the reasoning device of Comparison & Contrast in conjunction with Cause & Effect; this is the simplest and most effective approach. Had he not used this approach, the author's argument would most likely have come across as personal and subjective, and the reader would have assumed that the author had some sort of ulterior motive for defending the use of drones.

READING 2

Sample Essay 5

Student Jupiter
예비11, 2017 계관웅어학원 SAT 600B반

According to the passage "The virtue of Business: How markets Encourage Ethical Behavior", written by unnamed author, he claims that the business which treats customers and employees ethically earns more success comparing to others. The relationship between ethical behavior and business success is shown through John Mueller's primary example "Barnum & Bailey circus".

"Barnum and Bailey" is one of the greatest shows on Earth. However, it was unable to function with honesty since the customers ran a high risk of being cheated. As the author states this prior problem of the show, it allows readers to understand what the reality was before the change. The author cities the longtime Hollywood columnist "Jim Tully" in order to reveal corrupt acts of pretending: circuses pretend to be honest while exploiting innocent tubes.

In paragraph 3, the author strengthn his argument as the main idea is followed after more exemplification. The circus spokesman previously tried to inform audiences with probability of valuables getting stolen during the show. Disappointed by the reality, customers decreased significantly and therefore, Barnum & Bailey circus adapted changes in creating value for audiences. As the passage shows cause and effect relationship in passages, main claim tends to emphasize its importance. It also able readers to follow along with logical order of the happening.

After the attempts trying to create moral senses in the show, "Barnum & Bailey" has grown to be the dominant business model. Being ethical and honest was what both customers and owners were searching for and was a stepping stone for enjoyable, profitable circus. While the author used Barnum & Bailey as an example of evolution of ethical business, he is able to illustrate further reasoning for need of ethics and virtues in businesses. The author has created the mood shift from negative to positive as the circus achieved greater success and that once again reinforces the claim.

Good ethics lead to pleasant business matters. The author has taught readers the primary business strategy — honesty & good ethics — and it supports the idea "businesses gain a competitive advantage when they treat their customers and employees ethically". Long term relationship between customers and employees can only maintain through honest behaviors.

Problem 1:

Student Jupiter also failed to identify any of the author's rhetorical devices. This is a big problem, because it probably means that there is not much to look at in the main body. Remember that identifying the author's rhetorical devices is one of the best ways to draw attention of evaluators who do not have much time to analyze your essay thoroughly.

Problem 2:

This student made a very serious error simply by stating a "fact" that is not a fact. Student Jupiter claimed that "it was unable to function with honesty because the customers ran a high risk of being cheated." Unfortunately, this is not true; the author clearly stated that customers were cheated before B & B came along. Misrepresenting the author's intent in this manner would result in a score of less than 2.5 out of 4 for the reading.

Problem 3:

Student Jupiter used some awkward sentences such as "As the passage shows cause and effect relationship, the main claim tends to emphasize its importance." This is a terrible sentence for the following reasons.

First, there is no clear connection between the fact that the Cause & Effect was used and the argument that the importance of the main argument was emphasized.

Second, the main claim, by itself, cannot emphasize its importance. The author can emphasize the importance of the main claim.

Poorly-constructed sentences like this could easily cause the evaluator to ignore the rest of the essay. Students need to do a lot of hard work to master English grammar; unfortunately weak grammar and other related problems are not among the objectives of this book. This book is strictly about how to improve your analytical skills as a critic. Students with fundamental English problems must seek help elsewhere.

Problem 4:

In the last paragraph the student says "Good ethics lead to pleasant business." This is a very dangerous remark to make in this sort of essay; the student seems to be expressing his or her own opinion, but this essay is supposed to be a rhetorical analysis not a content analysis. In other words, nothing for or against the author's opinion can be stated. Never. The student could have said, "The main idea of the passage is that good ethics lead to pleasant business." Remember in any rhetorical critique, you can only discuss the author's rhetorical devices, not the content: examples, styles or reasoning devices.

According to the passage " The virtue of Business : How markets Encourage Ethical Behavior", written by unnamed author, he ¡claims that the business which treats customers and employees ethically ⟨earns more success⟩ comparing to others. The relationship between ethical behavior and business success is shown through John Mueller's primary example "Bamum & Bailey circus".

"Bamum and Bailey" ¡is one of the greatest shows on Earth. However, ⟨it was unable to function with honesty since the customers ran a high risk of being cheated.⟩ As the author states ≪this prior problem of the show, it allows≫. : readers to understand what the reality was before the change. The author cites the longtime Hollywood Columnist "Jim Tully" in order to reveal corrupt acts of pretending : circuses pretend to be honest while exploiting innocent tubes.

In a paragraph 3, the author strengthns this argument as the main idea is ⟨followed after⟩ more exemplification. The circus spokesman previously tried to inform audiences with probability of valuables getting stolen during the show. Disappointed by the reality, customers decreased significantly and therefore, Bamum & Bailey circus adapted changes in creating value for audiences. As the passage shows cause and effect relationship in passages, main claim tends to emphasize its importance. It also able readers to follow along with logical order of the happening.

After the attempts trying to create moral senses in the show, "Bamum & Bailey" has grown to be the dominant business model. ⟨Being ethical and honest was what both customers and owners were searching for and was a stepping stone for enjoyable, profitable circus?. While the author used an example of evolution of ethical business, he has Bamum & Bailey as shown his remarked importance his claim once again is able to illustrate further reasoning for need of ethics and virtues in businesses. It is the significant As The author has created the mood shift from negative to positive as the circus achieved greater success and that ~~reflects~~ once again reinforces the claim.

Good ethics lead to ~~Good busin~~ pleasant business matters. The author has taught readers the ~~importance of honesty and~~ el primary business strategy – honesty & good ethics – and ~~that~~ it supports the idea " businesses gain a competitive advantage when they treat their customers and employees ethically ". Long term relationship between customers and employees can only maintain through honest behaviors.

• Check if the sentences you wrote are understood the way you want them to be.   2.5/ 2.5/ 2.5

Sample Essay 6

Student Hibiscus
예비12, 2017 계관웅어학원 SAT 600B반

In "The Virtue of Business; How Markets Encourage Ethical Behavior," an anonymous writer builds an argument to persuade his audience that virtue is important to succeed business. The author uses example and reasoning to support his claim.

The author gains a idea from political scientist John Mueller that business gets advantage by treating customers and employees ethically and honestly. Then, he shows the example by Mueller, the Barnum & Bailey Circus. He says, "··· Barnum & Bailey created value for customers, ··· they convinced crowds to value and enjoy a visit to the circus." It shows the cause and effect of virtual business that if business is ethic and honest, it can get profit in the long term. His audience might imagine the situation when they pay for things or services. They would agree the writer's point by put themselves in the cases when they meet virtuous business and unethical business. Most people may prefer honest and ethical business, thus the writer could deliver his opinion effectively.

The author claims that if the business is not ethical, it would fail. He says, "What we learn from the evolution in the treatment of circus customers is that unethical behavior in the free market causes companies to fail." It sounds reasonable that unethical business is doomed to fail because the ethical business succeeds by virtues. However, this assertion is too extreme and does not have any evidence to persuade the audience. There might be company which is unethical but successful. Moreover, no evidence can cause the doubt by the audience because they may think his claim is just an opinion, not a fact. Thus, his last two sentences in the passage are not persuasive and truly reasonable.

By using example and reasoning, the author builds an argument to persuade his audience that businesses gain a competitive advantage when they treat their customers and employees ethically, but somewhat ineffective to deliver his claim.

Problem 1:

Student Hibiscus only mentioned reasoning and example instead of identifying the author's rhetorical devices. Mentioning "reasoning and example" is as bad as not mentioning anything at all. For the reasons explained above, failing to identify the author's rhetorical devices in the introduction causes serious problems in the following main body.

Problem 2:

In the second paragraph student Hibiscus abruptly mentions "cause and effect" without elaborating on it; as explained above, Cause & Effect should have been identified in the introduction and should have been expanded upon in the main body. Finally, the student should have explained why Cause & Effect was effective in conveying the author's central idea.

Problem 3:

In the third paragraph the student states "However, this assertion was too extreme and does not have evidence to persuade the audience." There is nothing wrong with this argument by itself. However, the problem is that we, the readers of this essay, are not sure if this student's intent is to give a positive assessment of the reading or to criticize it. Before or after this critical remark, the student should have made clear what the general purpose of this essay was.

In " The Virtue of Business: How Markets Encourage Ethical Behavior," an anonymous writer builds an argument, to persuade his audience that (virtue) is important to succeed ᵢₙ business. The author uses example and reasoning to support his claim.
Vague

The author gains ⓐ ᵃⁿ idea from political scientist John Mueller that business gets advantage by treating customers and employees ethically and honestly. Then, «he shows the example by Mueller, the Barnum & Bailey Circus» ᴳᵒᵒᵈ He says, "... Barnum & Bailey created value for customers. ... they convinced crowds to value and enjoy a visit to the circus." It shows the cause and effect of virtual business that if business is ethic and honest, it can get profit in the long term. His audience might imagine the situation when they pay for things or services. They would agree the writer's point by put themselves in the cases When they meet virtous business and unethical business. Most people may prefer honest and ethical business, thus the writer could deliever his opinion effectively.

The author claims that if the business is not ethical, it would fail. He says, "What we learn from the evolution in the treatment of Circus customers is that unethical behavior in the free market causes companies to fail." It sounds reasonable that unethical business is doomed to fail because the ethical business succeeds by virtues. «However, this assertion is too extreme and does not have any evidence to persuade the audience» There might be ⓐ a company which is unethical but successful. Moreover, no evidence can cause the doubt by the audience because they may think his claim is just an opinion, not a fact. Thus, his last two sentences in the passage are not persuative and truely reasonable. *Present the idea in the beginning of the paragraph. Your readers don't always read the whole passage*

→

By using example and reasoning, the author builds
an argument to persuade his audience that businesses
gain a competitive advantage when they treat their customers
and employees ethically, but somewhat uneffective to deliver
his claim.

· Try to replace words "get" & "things"
b/c they are very casual & vague!

3.5/ 2.5 /3

NEW SAT
ESSAY
PREP
SAT
ESSAY
PREP

Sample Essay 7

Student Kalahari
예비11, 2017 계관웅어학원 SAT 600B반

The primary goal for companies is usually benefits. The nameless author of article "The virtue of Business: How Markets Encourage Ethical Behavior" expands on a particular sector of this idea, stating that businesses should follow the norm — treating customers and employees ethically — in order to gain competitive advantages. To effectively persuade his readers, the author offers a stark contrast and appeals to the readers' emotion.

To begin with, the author inserts a stark contrast of two periods of the circus Barnum & Bailey. The first period is when it "functioned dishonestly," which the "customers ⋯ ran a high risk of being cheated:" "ticket takers would short-change them ⋯, pickpockets were paid commissions to roam the grounds and victimize customers ⋯, circus sideshows were tacky; and games were impossible to win⋯." To the readers, this place would seem like it is "composed of evil." They would have no incentives to attend this circus, and they're right — "customers soon stopped attending." However, the author then illustrates the changes of Barnum & Bailey Circus in chronological order. This second period is when the circus treated employees and customers ethically — "they worked hard to change negative impressions of circuses and to attract new customers." Consequently, it produced the "greatest show on earth," and their strategy became the consensus and the norm. This will come as a shock for the readers, as they will be surprised by the rapid evolution of a company which was once the worst case possibly imagined. Therefore, this simple but sharp comparison and contrast, depending on the fact of wheter the business treated customers and employees ethically or not, clearly represents how "profitable" this method is. The author will successfully strengthen his central idea as the readers easily grasp the usefulness of this economic strategy from this stark contrast.

In addition, the author appeals to the readers' emotion. Like the author mentioned, customers have no interest in the business strategy. "They came because their enjoyment was worth the money paid." The question does this business treat us ethically and honestly is the fundamental rubric of how people judge a company, a business, or and entertainment. Businesses must satiate the consumers because it is the only way they can gain profits and suceed. Hence, just looking at the author's main idea alone, the readers will nod in agreement because he is talking about the obvious — it's the underlying reason why they would buy something. Therefore, that businesses gain a competitive advantage when they treat their customers and employees ethically becomes a undeniable fact.

The anonymous writer of "The Virtue of Business: How Markets Encourage Ethical Behavior" is able to draw support from his readers through his implication of clear contrast and with the appeal to the readers' self interest.

Problem 1:

Unfortunately, student Kalahari identified only one reasoning device, "stark contrast". However, as mentioned earlier, an author, who uses reasoning devices to support a subjective central idea such as this, would probably like to come across as more objective. In such a situation, it would be wise for the author to use as many reasoning devices as possible, including Comparison & Contrast and Cause & Effect. The passage analyzed here is not an exception. With a little more attention and effort the student should have been able to identify "Circuses that practiced deception often earned quick profit, but their success was short lived. Disappointed and suspicious, customers soon stopped coming." as a cause and also identify "But in1880 Barnum and Bailey Circus set in motion a variety of changes." as the corresponding effect.

Problem 2:

At the beginning of the second paragraph this student made a critical mistake by saying "··· stark contrast of two periods ··· the first period ··· functioned dishonestly ···." However, the given reading clearly states, "Prior to the founding of Barnum and Bailey Circus ··· circuses functioned dishonestly." In other words, Barnum and Bailey Circus never functioned dishonestly. This kind of misunderstanding ruins the integrity of the entire essay.

Problem 3:

One of the analytical elements identified by the student, appealing to emotion, didn't work at all. The third paragraph, the one dealing with an emotional approach, doesn't make sense. "Business must satiate customers because it is the only way they can gain profit and succeed" First of all, this is not the author's argument. At least, student Kalahari doesn't say that it is the author's argument. So where did this idea come from? If an essay does not attribute an idea to a specific person, then the reader will automatically regarded that idea as belonging to whoever wrote it. In this case that would be the student. Second of all, how is this related to emotions? In conclusion, this is not a rhetorical analysis.

The primary goal for companies is usually benefits. The nameless author of article "The Virtue of Business: How Markets Encourage Ethical Behavior" expands on a particular sector of this idea, stating that businesses should follow the norm — treating customers and employees ethically — in order to gain competitive advantages. To effectively ~~convince~~ persuade his readers, the author offers a stark contrast and appeals to the readers' emotion. *profit*

before & after B&B?

To begin with, the author inserts a stark contrast of «two periods of the circus Barnum & Bailey. The first period is ~~where they~~ ^when it^ "functioned dishonestly" which ~~it~~ the "customers... ran a high risk of being cheated:" "ticket takers would short-change ~~them~~ them...., pickpockets were paid commissions to ~~an~~ roam the grounds and victimize customers,..., circus sideshows were tacky; and games were impossible to win..." To the readers, this place would ~~as~~ seem like it is "composed of evil." They would have no incentives to attend this circus, and they're right — "customers soon stopped attending." However, ~~a~~ the author then illustrates the changes of Barnum & Bailey Circus in chronological order. This second period is when the circus treated employees and customers ethically — "they worked hard to change negative impressions of circuses and to attract new ~~cus~~ customers." Consequently, ~~they~~ ^it^ produced the "greatest show on earth," and their strategy became the consensus and the norm. This will come as a shock for the readers, as they will be surprised by the rapid evolution of a company which was ~~at~~ once the worst case possibly imagined. Therefore, this simple but sharp comparison and contrast, depending on the ~~method~~ ^fact^ of the business treat~~ing~~ed ^whether^ customers and employees ethically or not, clearly represents how "profitable" this method is. The author will successfully strengthen his central idea as the readers easily grasp the usefulness of this economic strategy from this ~~sharp~~ ^stark^ contrast.

Barnum & Bailey's began clean.

~~Also~~ In addition, the author appeals to the readers' emotion. Like the author ^mentioned^ ~~said~~, customers ~~and~~ ~~employees~~ a have no interest in the business strategy. "They came because their enjoyment was worth the money paid." ~~Whether the has~~ The question #does this business treat us ethically and honestly is the fundamental ~~a~~ rubric of how people judge a company, a business, ~~or~~ an entertainment. Businesses must satiate the consumers ~~&~~ ~~the~~ because it is the only way they can gain profits and succeed. Hence, just looking at the author's main idea alone, the readers will nod in agreement because he is talking about the obvious — it's the ~~fund~~ underlying reason why they would buy something. Therefore, ~~&~~ that ^those^ businesses gain a competitive advantage when they treat their customers and employees ethically becomes (a) ^an^ undeniable fact.

The anonymous writer of "The Virtue of Business: How Markets Encourage Ethical Behavior" is able to draw support from his readers through his implication of clear contrast and with the appeal to the readers' self interest.

Beating around the bush? I don't see the point.
⊕ How is the author appealing to emotion?

2.5/2.5/3

Sample Essay 8

Student Raptor
예비10, 2017 계관웅어학원 SAT 600B반

The writer of "The Virtue of Business: How Markets Encourage Ethical Behavior" claims that long-term business success is in porportion to to ethical behavior. He compares specific examples to illustrate his statements, further strengthening the persuasiveness of his essay.

Before providing business models, Anonymous, the writer, first mentions an authority. The writer uses John Mueller to bring his own claim. By introducing an authority who is in agreement with the writer's main argument, the writer increases the credibility of this passage. The effect of mentioning a familiar figure can cause the audience to be more easily persuaded. After that, the writer uses the example John Mueller set out as his own. The writer first introduces the examples of businesses that "functioned dishonestly". He claims that although "Circuses that practiced deception often earned quick profits, but their success was short-lived". After showing a bad business strategy, the author shows a better business model relative to prior one. Barnum & Bailey Circus, the embodiment that validates the author's theory, uses methods that are exactly opposite of previous circuses. The writers explains the reason for Barnum & Bailey Circus' success and gives an stark contrast between previous businesses. The writer continues, describing the consumers' behaviors toward the virtues of Business. By effectively comparing two different styles of businesses with the addition of the consumer's response, Anonymous shows evidently the superiority and effectiveness of businesses that concentrated on virtues. The writer concludes with "Unethical businesses trying to prosper in a market where good ethics are the norm, are doomed to fail" showing how "good ethics" strategy predominates the US, emphasizing the competitive advantage of ethical behavior once more.

Throughout the passage, the writer uses examples that correspond with his stance. Anonymous' effective usage of comparisons between examples proved to be a solid evidences that increased the overall persuasiveness of his essay.

Problem 1:

Again, this student only identified "comparison" as the author's reasoning device. However, as mentioned earlier, an author who uses reasoning devices to support a subjective central idea such as this would probably like to come across as more objective. In such a situation it would be wise for the author to use as many reasoning devices as possible, including Comparison & Contrast and Cause & Effect. The reading analyzed here is not an exception. With a little more attention and effort student Raptor should have been able to identify "Circuses that practiced deception often earned quick profit, but their success was short lived. Disappointed and suspicious, customers soon stopped coming." as a cause and also identify "But in1880 Barnum and Bailey Circus set in motion a variety of changes." as the corresponding effect. Additionally, student Raptor argues that the author "compares specific examples ···," but the author did not use this reasoning device based on Comparison & Contrast just to compare examples.

Problem 2:

Student Raptor failed to elaborate on what he or she had identified in the introduction, so the main body seems separate and unrelated to the introduction. Consequently, the entire essay lacks continuity and seems underdeveloped.

Problem 3:

This student made arguments without offering significant

support. For example, the student argues "··· effective comparisons between examples proved to be a solid evidences," but then fails to point out any comparison between examples or indicate the reason why they are assumed to be solid. Also, comparisons between examples cannot be called evidence.

The writer of "The Virtue of Business: How Markets Encourage Ethical Behavior" claims that long-term business success is in portportion to [spell] to ethical behavior. He compares specific examples to illustrate his statements, further strengthening the persuasiveness of his essay. (not quantitative...) [Compares ex...?]

(X) «Before providing business models, Anonymous, the writer, first mentions an authority. The writer uses John Mueller to bring his own claim. By introducing an authority who is in agreement with the writer's main argument, the writer increases the credibility of this passage. The effect of mentioning a familiar figure can cause the audience to be more easily persuaded.»

After that, the writer uses the example John Mueller set out as his own. The writer first introduces the examples of businessess that "functioned dishonestly". He claims that although "Circuses that practiced deception often earned quick profits, but their success was short-lived". After showing a bad business strategy, the author shows a better business model relative to prior one. Barnum & Bailey Circus, the embodiment that validates the author's theory, uses methods that are exactly opposite of previous circuses. The writers explains the reason for Barnum & Bailey Circus' success and gives an stark contrast between previous businesses. The writer continues, describing the consumers' behaviors toward the virtues of Business. By effectively comparing two different styles of businesses, with the addition of the consumer's response, Anonymous shows evidently the superiority and effectiveness of businessess that concentrated on virtues. The writer concludes with "Unethical businesses trying to prosper in a market where good ethics are the norm, are doomed to fail" showing how "good ethics" strategy predominates the US, emphasizing the competitive advantage of ethical behavior once more.   What is it?

Throughout the passage, the writer uses examples that corresponds with his stance. Anonymous' effective usage of comparisons between examples proved to be a

Solid evidence(s) that increased the ~~overall~~ persuasiveness of his essay. (officially) uncountable

- ⊗ The four sentences are the same. Delete all.
- Divide the paragraph. Let your ideas show.

3 / 2.5 / 3.5

An Improved Version
of Sample Essay 8
for achieving the maximum score

The author of "The Virtue of Business: How Markets Encourage Ethical Behavior" claims that long-term business success is achieved in proportion to the ethical behavior of the business operator. The author compares and contrasts very specific examples that are to-the-point and that illustrate how these differences support the central idea. This strengthens the persuasiveness of the essay, which is well integrated with the other analytical device, Cause & Effect.

Before providing business models, the anonymous author first mentions an authority figure, John Mueller, and uses his writings to back up the author's own claim. By introducing an authority figure who is in agreement with the author's main argument, the author increases the credibility of this passage. This is necessary because the central idea could easily be perceived as outdated and a cliché, or just the author's personal opinion. Therefore, the author found it necessary to point out that he/she was not the only one who had this idea. The author goes one step further by making use of the same example used by John Mueller. The author first introduces examples of businesses that are "functioned dishonestly". The author starts off by stating that although "Circuses that practiced deception often earned quick profits··· their success was short-lived" in order to establishes a clear example that will be sharply contrasted later in the passage. After pointing out a bad business strategy, the author introduces a better model, in order to provide a stark contrast between the two models, which eventually leads to the author's central idea. Barnum & Bailey Circus, the embodiment that validates the author's theory, uses methods that are the exact opposite of the previously-mentioned circuses. In order to corroborate the central idea, the author continues by describing the behavior of consumers toward the virtues of Business; the cause, the ethical business strategy, produced an effect, the consumers' positive response. Combining Comparison & Contrast and Cause & Effect is always a winning recipe in this kind of argument which can often be considered either too personal or a bit of a cliché. By effectively comparing the two different styles of businesses with the addition of the consumer's response, the anonymous author clearly illustrates the superiority and effectiveness of businesses that concentrated on virtues. The author concludes by stating "Unethical businesses trying to prosper in a market where good ethics are the norm, are doomed to fail" showing how strategies based on "good ethics" predominate in the U.S., once more emphasizing the competitive advantage of ethical behavior.

Throughout the passage, the reader is provided with critical examples that correspond directly with the author's point of view. The effective use of Comparisons & Contrast between self-explanatory examples proves to be a solid rhetorical approach that raises the overall persuasiveness of the argument to higher level.

READING 3

N E W S S A T
E S S A Y
P R E P
S A T
E S S A Y
P R E P

NEW SAT ESSAY PREP

Sample Essay 9

Student Abyss
고2, 2017 계관웅어학원 SAT advanced반

By referring studies from experts, introducing contradicting theories, and constantly exemplifying his claims, Benedict Cary strengthens his argument that in the development of certain skills, uncertainty remains whether practice or native talent is more important.

Firstly, he increases validity of his argument by consistently exemplifying his ideas. In paragraph 1, he catches attention of readers by starting the essay with common question raised by public. It not only concentrates the readers but makes readers to imagine the given situation, which can lead to the effect of readers logically answering the question by themselves. It makes readers easier to eventually reach the conclusion author suggested: uncertain. Also, in paragraph 10, when addressing factors determining the performance of a person in certain area, author brought example of violin, basketball, and language to make readers to understand his claim. He uses example of person grown up in bilingual household, effectively demonstrating the effect of age in performance.

Secondly, his claims are mostly based on studies of professionals, which makes his argument credible. In paragraph 3, 4, 5, 6, 7, 8, 11, 12,

13, he used ideas of Dr. Ericsson and Zach Hambrick and extended them with his ideas. He intentionally introduced details about those professionals, like "psychologist now at Florida State University" and "a Michigan State University" to illustrate that the ideas he adapted in his essay are logically valid and socially, academically credible, eventually adding persuasiveness to his essay.

Thirdly, to effectively prove his conclusion that way certain skills develop is uncertain, he introduces both contradicting theories toward the subject, to prove his essay's objectivity and validity. In paragraph 3, he cited the research of K. Andres Ericsson, who argued that practice time is certainly more significant than the inherent ability. He supports this idea in paragraph 8 by showing existence of truly elite performances. However, in the same time, author introduces theory by Dr. Hambrick, which says that only 25% ~ 4% of practice could contribute to performance. By showing both theories are logical and possibly be true, he eventually makes readers to think that there is no fixed answer for this argument. He also raises effect of showing that he is unbiased, by refuting two researches, with totally different ideas.

In conclusion, by referring ideas of experts, using examples, refuting two opposite theories, author supported his argument and made it persuasive.

Problem 1:

Like so many others, student Abyss also failed to identify any of the author's rhetorical devices, which is a recurring and very serious problem. As explained before, many authors resort to various kinds of objective devices in order to support their subjective central ideas, and an effective way for them to do this is by using Comparison & Contrast and Cause & Effect. So always bear in mind that, whatever the central idea is, looking for these reasoning devices should be your first step when analyzing any given reading, and this particular reading is no exception.

Problem 2:

The student mentioned the effect of a question used at the beginning of the given reading, but right before doing so, talked about effective exemplification. This is a problem because there is no connection between those two explanations or arguments; they have nothing to do with each other. A question is not an exemplification. Those two explanations are irrelevant. Right after making arguments on exemplification, you need to provide a relevant example of exemplification and then go on to the discussion of the question.

Problem 3:

In paragraph four student Abyss uses the word "prove" twice. *Prove* is a very strong word, and what the author of the given reading was providing was not proof or evidence, but just arguments. A theory proves nothing; it can only present arguments in favor of an idea or at best support an idea. This student appears to have problems with fundamental concepts.

By referring from experts, introducing contradicting theories, and constantly exemplifying his claims, Benedict Carey strengthens his argument that in the development of certain skills, uncertainty remains whether practice or native talent is more importan -t.

+ cause & effect / comparison & contrast

Firstly, he increases validity of his argument by consistently exemplifying his ideas. In paragraph 1, he catches attention of readers by starting the essay with common question raised by public. It not only concentrates the readers but makes readers to imagine the given situation, which can lead to the effect of readers logically answering the question by themselves. It makes readers easier to eventually reach the conclusion author suggested: uncertain. Also, in paragraph 10, when addressing factors determining the performance of a person in certain area, author brought example of violin, basketball, and language to make readers easier to understand his claim. He uses example of person grown up in bilingual household, effectively demonstrating the effect of age in performance.

Secondly, his claims are mostly based on ~~argum~~ studies of professionals, which makes his argument credible. In paragraph 3, 4, 5, 6, 7, 8, 11, 12, 13, he used ideas of Dr. Ericsson and Zach Hambrick and extended them with his ideas. He intentionally introduced details about those professionals, like "psychologist now at Florida state University" and "a Michigan State University" to illustrate that the ideas he adapted in his essay are logically valid and socially, academically credible, eventually adding persuasiveness to his essay.

Thirdly, to effectively prove his conclusion that certain skills develop is uncertain, he introduces both contradicting (way) theories toward the subjects to prove his objectivity and validity. In paragraph 3, he cited the research of K. Andres (essays) Ericsson, who argued that practice time is certainly more significant than the inherent ability. He supports this idea in paragraph 8, 10 by showing existence of truly elite performances. However, in the same time, author introduces theory by Dr. Hambrick, which says that only 25% of 4% of practice could contribute to performance. By showing both theories are logical and possibly be true, he eventually makes readers to think that there is no fixed answer for this argument. He also raises effect of showing that he is unbiased, by carefully two researches, with totally different ideas.

In conclusion, by ~~the~~ retelling ideas of experts, using examples, refuting two opposite theories, author supported his argument and made it persuasive.

Because you ~~miss~~ failed to identify two outstanding $ reasoning devices that the author used, the entire essay turns rather dull and ineffective.

$$3 / 1.5 / 3 = 7.5 \times 2 = 15/24$$

NEW SAT
ESSAY
PREP
SAT
ESSAY
PREP

Sample Essay 10

Student Blue Whale
예비11, 2017 계관웅어학원 SAT advanced반

In the passage, Benedict Cary builds his argument that in developing certain skills, whether practice or natural talent is more important still remains unknown. The author uses studies and stylistic elements to persuade the audience.

First of all, Cary gives many examples of studies about "contributions of practice and native talent to the development of elite performance." The first example he gives is a research by K. Andres Ericsson about musicians. This research concluded that practice time explained about 80 percent difference between elite performers and amateurs. Another example the author gives is a new paper by Zach Hambrick that came out with different conclusion. By using 88 studies, he estimated that there was only about 20-25 percent of difference in performance in music, sports and games, and only 4 percent in academics. The author, Cary, uses two opposite examples of study to effectively emphasize the point that it is hard to conclude whether effort or talent is more important in skill building. Cary also says "the range of findings and level of disagreement are themselves hints that there are likely to be factors involved in building expertise that are neither genetic nor related to the amount of practice time." He gives a new possibility to the debate that neither of the two is important.

Furthermore, Cary employs stylistic elements to persuade the audience. In the second paragraph, the author asks questions such as "How good can I get? How much time will it take? Is it possible I'm a natural at this? What's the percentage in this exactly?". These questions are rhetorical that the author is asking not to get answers but to make the audience think about the questions and emphasize the main argument of the passage. In this way, the audience can redeem the answers of the questions. Another stylistic element Cary uses is quotes. Quotes are repeatedly used throughout the passage to cite the words of the researchers and scientists. For instance, ""We found that, yes, practice is important, and of course it's absolutely necessary to achieve expertise," said Hambrick".

Problem 1:

"Stylistic elements" can mean many things. Student Blue Whale again did not identify any of the author's rhetorical devices, which is a recurring and very serious problem, as I explained many times before. Read the comments for the previous essays very carefully.

Problem 2:

At the beginning of the second paragraph the student makes reference to several difference examples, but in the introduction failed to even mention exemplification. Therefore, there is no continuity between the introduction and the beginning of the second paragraph. The introduction is not connected to the main body. This essay is not properly developed.

Problem 3:

Student Blue Whale argues that the author used a Rhetorical Question as a stylistic element. This should have been mentioned in the introduction. The student claims that this Rhetorical Question is effective, but fails to explain why this Rhetorical Question is effective in conveying the central idea.

Problem 4:

The student claims that quotes are another stylistic element used by the author, but quotes are a type of example or evidence, not a stylistic element. Misidentifications of this sort are sure to result in the student getting a lower the score.

In the passage, Benedict Cary builds his argument that in developing certain skills, whether practice or natural ~~talent~~ is more important still remains unknown. The author uses studies and stylistic ~~en~~ elements to persuade the audience.

Not specific at all

First of all, Cary gives many examples of studies about "contributions of practice and native talent to the development of elite performance." The first example he gives is a research by K. Anders Ericsson about musicians. This research concluded that ~~about the percent of~~ practice time explained about 80 percent difference between elite performers and amateurs. Another example the author gives is a new paper by Zach Hambrick that came out with different conclusion. By using 88 studies, he estimated ~~about~~ that there was only 20-25 percent of difference in performance in music, sports and games, and only 4 percent in academics. The author, Cary, uses two opposite examples of study to effectively emphasize the point that it is hard to conclude whether effort or talent is more important in skill building. Cary also says "the range of findings and level of disagreement are themselves hints that there are likely to be factors involved in building expertise that are neither genetic nor related to the amount of practice time." He gives a new possibility to the debate that neither of the two is important.

Furthermore, Cary employs stylistic elements to persuade the audience. In the second paragraph, the author asks questions such as "How good can I get? How much time will it take? Is it possible I'm a natural at this? What's the percentage in this, exactly?". These questions are rhetorical that the author is asking not ~~to~~ to get answers but to make the audience think ~~again~~ about the questions and emphasize the main argument of the passage. In this way, the audience can ~~redeem~~ the answers of the questions. ~~Another~~ Another stylistic element Cary uses is quotes. Quotes are repeatedly used throughout the passage to cite the words of the researchers and scientists. For instance, "We found that, yes, practice is important, and of course it's absolutely necessary to achieve expertise," said Hambrick"

You totally ignored the class instructions all together as if you hadn't taken the class; How unfortunate.

$$3(1/3 = 7 \times 2 = 14/20$$

Sample Essay 11

Student Pacific
고2, 2017 계관웅어학원 SAT advanced반

Benedict Cary writes a report on whether practice or native talent is more important. Rather than providing an exact answer to this prolonged topic of debate, he claims that uncertainty remains. Cary strengthens the logic and persuasiveness of his argument through the use of reliable sources, statistics, and effective transitions between paragraphs.

Throughout the essay, different perspectives are included regarding one particular issue. Since the essay does not stick itself to one side, and includes lack of supporting details to strengthen each main idea, the audience may question the validity of the context. In order to prevent this risk, the author mentions the source of information beforehand. For instance, "Ericsson, a psychologist now at Florida state University", "Hambrick, a Michigan state University psychologist." are inserted. As a result, despite the fact that the two completely contrasting ideas are argued, the readers are able to provide each point of argument an equal sense of trust. Moreover, the reason why Cary successfully strengthens his ideas even with minimal amount of explanation is because of the use of statistics "Compiling results from 88 studies across ⋯ 20 percent to 25 percent" "the number is much lower — 4 percent." People are easily attracted to numbers as they act as a piece of evidence that proves that their source is accurate.

As mentioned before, the author gives various, potential factors that might contribute to the development of certain skills such as practice, talent, age, personality, pressure and much more. Including a large number of ideas in one piece of work has the risk of disturbing the general flow of the passage, decreasing the concentration of the readers. However Benedic Cary overcomes this by inserting phrases and quotes in the beginning of a new paragraph that naturally connects with the previous context. As an example, "One of those people", "But his own studies" ⋯ etc are used. To be more specific, paragraph 9 serves as a transition from talent and practice to factors such as age and personality. "Yet the range of findings and level of disagreement ⋯ there are likely to be factors ⋯ that are neither genetic nor related to the amount of practice time." Immediately the next paragraphs starts with "One is the age ⋯". Thus the effective transitions between paragraphs made the essay seem united and connected even though it contained irrelevant concepts.

Be it the impact of authority or transitions, there is no doubt.

Problem 1:

In the introduction student Pacific argues that the author "strengthens logic and persuasiveness ⋯ through statistics, effective transitions ⋯." But the author clearly used two strong reasoning devices: Cause & Effect and Comparison & Contrast. As I stresses numerous times before, the first thing you must do when analyzing a reading on an SAT test is look for these two reasoning devices.

Problem 2:

At the beginning of the second paragraph student Pacific makes an argument which does not make sense. "Since the essay doesn't stick itself to one side, and includes lack of details to support each main idea ⋯ the audience may question the validity of the context."; this doesn't make any sense at all. First of all, "each main idea" implies that there are several main ideas and this is nonsense, because an essay has only one main idea. Second, readers obviously take an interest in the validity of the central idea, but nobody cares about "the validity of the context". Using this sort of expression in this context is not only meaningless but strongly suggests that that this student was either not thinking deeply enough or is not proficient enough in English to tackle rhetorical analysis.

Problem 3:

The student should have explained how the author's use of statistics was effective in supporting the central idea.

Problem 4:

In the last paragraph, student Pacific did it again: what he or she did in the second paragraph was making an argument that is so confusing and meaningless. By inserting one phrase, student Pacific claims that the author overcame diversion he or she created by providing so many ideas. For the above arguments to have any validity at all, the student must explain how, but this student made no effort to explain.

How do you know this? : conjecture

Benedict Cary writes a report on whether practice or native talent is more important. Rather than providing an exact answer to this prolonged topic of debate, he claims that uncertainty remains. Cary strengthens the logic and persuasiveness of his argument through the use of reliable sources, statistics, and effective transitions between paragraphs. *+ comparison & contrast and cause & effect*

Throughout the essay, different perspectives are included regarding one particular issue. Since the essay does not stick itself to one side, and includes lack of supporting details to strengthen each main idea, the audience may question the validity of the context. In order to prevent this risk, the author mentions the source of information beforehand. For instance, "Ericsson, a psychologist now at Florida State University", "Hambrick, a Michigan State University psychologist" are inserted. As a result, despite the fact that the two completely contrasting ideas are argued, the readers are able to provide each point of argument an equal sense of trust. Moreover, the reason why Cary successfully strengthens his ideas even with minimal amount of explanation is because of the use of statistics "Compiling results from 88 studies across... 20 percent to 25 percent" "the number is much lower—4 percent." People are easily attracted to numbers as they act as a piece of evidence that proves that their source is accurate.

As mentioned before, the author gives various, potential factors that might contribute to the development of certain skills such as practice, talent, age, personality, pressure and much more. Including a large number of ideas in one piece of work. has the risk of disturbing the general flow of the passage, decreasing the concentration of the readers. However, Benedict Cary overcomes this by inserting phrases and quotes. in the beginning of a new paragraph that naturally connects with the previous context. As an example, "one of those people", "But his own studies"... etc are used. To be more specific, paragraph 9 serves as a transition from talent and practice to factors such as age and personality. "Yet the range of findings and level of disagreement ... there are likely to be factors ... that are neither genetic nor related to the amount of practice time." Immediately the next paragraphs starts with "One is the age...". Thus the effective transitions between paragraphs made the essay seem united and connected even though it contained irrelevant concepts.

Be it the impact of authority or transitions, there is no doubt

Since you miss two outstanding devices that the author used, the rest of the essay fell short of being an effective analysis; too bad.

3/2/3.5 = 8.5×2 = 17/ 2

Sample Essay **12**

Student Atlantic
고2, 2017 계관웅어학원 SAT advanced반

Benedict Carey argues that during the development of certain skills, it is not evident whether practice or native talent is more important. In order to strengthen his argument, the author uses scientific examples and effective reasoning based on direct and powerful and contrast.

Through the argumentative technique of providing scientific examples, the passage author promotes a thesis regarding. Benedict Carey lists various studies conducted by different scientists: K. Anders Ecricsson, Zach Hambrick and Dr. Ecricsson. A 1993 study of musicians directed by K. Anders Edicsson figured out that practice time explains almost all the difference between elite performers and committed amateurs. A new experiment done by Zach Hambrick estimates that practice time can only explain about 20 to 25 percent of the difference between elite performers and committed amateurs. Zach Hambrick emphasized the point that practice time does not affect that much as many people have been saying. Dr. Ecricsson points out that there are going to be factors involved in building expertise that are neither genetic nor related with practice time. Thus, he lists the factors: the age at which a person starts, isolated practice and pressure. By accomodating different scientic examples, Benedict Carey's argument becomes more persuasive because scientific examples are trust-worthy and the different results of experiments back-up Benedict Carey's claim.

Scientific examples aside, another argumentative technique of direct and powerful compare and contrast also substantiates the author's claim. Compare and contrast can be seen between the outcome of K. Anders Ecricsson's experiment and Zach Hambrick's experiment. While K. Anders Ecricsson's study conveyed that practice time is the main factor that influences the development of a person, Zach Hambrick's new research argues that practice time only affects the development by 20 to 25 percent and the number is much lower in academics. Zach Hambrick quotes "practice time is not as important as many people have been saying." Even though, Zach Hambrick denies the claim that practice time is the main factor to influence the development, Zach Hambrick still does agree that practice time is important and is absolutely necessary to achieve expertise. The only contrast is that K. Anders Ecricsson focuses on practice time but Zach Hambrick focuses more to inborn gifts, in other words, native talent. As Benedict Carey presents a compare and contrast through the result of researches, it emphasizes Benedict Carey's claim because It clearly shows that during the development of certain skills, it is not evident whether practice time or native talent is the major factor.

Benedict Carey shows uncertainty on which, factor affects the most in deciding the development of certain skills — native talent or practice time. Without the use of scientific examples and direct and powerful compare and contrast, the author would have had a hard time conveying his opinion.

Problem 1:

In the introduction student Atlantic says "powerful compare and contrast". This is an unfortunate choice of words because compare is a verb; the student should have used Comparison & Contrast. Additionally, the student failed to identify Cause & Effect. This is a recurring problem. Please read the previous comments again.

Problem 2:

In the second paragraph the student mentions "argumentative technique", but providing scientific examples is not an argumentative technique. In the same paragraph he or she argues that using various examples is helpful to convey the author's central idea, but fails to explain why. Remember that every argument must be supported by proper explanation.

Problem 3:

Even though Comparison & Contrast is correctly identified in the third paragraph, nowhere, either in this paragraph or in the rest of the essay, does the student expand on why it is effective in conveying the central idea. Identifying the author's rhetorical devices is important, but it is not everything; you must explain why these rhetorical devices are effective in conveying the central idea.

Comparison

Benedict Carey argues that during the development of certain skills, it is not evident whether practice or native talent is more important. In order to strengthen his argument, the author uses scientific examples and effective reasoning based on direct and powerful compare and contrast. *Not specific enough*

    Through the argumentative technique of providing scientific examples, the passage author promotes a thesis regarding. Benedict Carey lists various studies conducted by different scientists: K. Anders Ecricsson, Zach Hambrick and Dr. Ecricsson. A 1993 study of musicians directed by K. Anders Edicsson figured out that practice time explains almost all the difference between elite performers and committed amateurs A new experiment done by Zach Hambrick estimates that practice time can only explain about 20 to 25 percent of the difference between elite performers and committed amateurs. Zach Hambrick emphasized the point that practice time does not affect that much as many people have been saying Dr. Ecricsson points out that there are going to be factors involved in building expertise that are neither genetic nor related with practice time Thus, he lists the factors: the age at which a person starts, isolated practice and pressure By accomodating different scientic examples, Benedict Carey's argument becomes more persuasive because scientific examples are trust-worthy and the different results of experiments back-up Benedict Carey's claim

    Scientific examples aside, another argumentative technique of direct and powerful compare and contrast also substantiates the author's claim. Compare and contrast can be seen between the outcome of K. Anders Ecricsson's experiment and Zach Hambrick's experiment. While, K. Anders Ecricsson's study conveyed that practice time is the main factor that influences the development of a person, Zach Hambrick's new research argues that practice time only affects the development by 20 to 25 percent and the number is much lower in academics. Zach Hambrick quotes. " practice time is not as important as many people have been saying." Even though, Zach Hambrick denies the claim that practice time is the main factor to influence the development, Zach Hambrick still does agree that practice time is important and is absolutely necessary to achieve expertise The only contrast   is that K. Anders Ecricsson focuses on practice time but Zach Hambrick focuses more to inborn gifts, in other words, native talent As Benedict Carey presents a compare and contrast through the result of researches, it emphasizes Benedict Carey's claim because it clearly shows that during the development of certain skills, it is not evident whether practice time or native talent is the major factor.

   Benedict Carey shows uncertainty on which factor affects the most in deciding the development of certain skills — native talent or practice time. Without the use of scientific examples and direct and powerful compare and contrast, the author would have had a hard time conveying his opinion.

How many times was it said in class
that compare & contrast is not an expression?
; You totally ignored class instructions
; read them very carefully over and over again

$$3 / 0.5 / 3 = 6.5 \times 2 = 13/20$$

An Improved Version
of Sample Essay 12
for achieving the maximum score

Benedict Carey argues that it is not evident whether practice or native talent is the more important factor in a person's effort to develop certain skills. In order to strengthen his argument, the author uses scientific examples and effective reasoning based on direct and powerful Comparison & Contrast.

By providing scientific examples as well as using argumentative techniques, the author of the passage promotes a thesis regarding the development of certain skills. Benedict Carey lists several studies conducted by various scientists: K. Anders Ericsson, Zach Hambrick. It is important to note that the number of these studies alone provides substantial support for the author's argument. A 1993 study of musicians directed by K. Anders Ericsson helped determine that practice time explains almost all the difference between elite professional performers and dedicated amateurs. A more recent experiment conducted by Zach Hambrick determined that practice time can only explain about 20 to 25 percent of the difference between elite professional performers and dedicated amateurs. A study by Zach Hambrick indicated that practice time was not as important as many people had thought. Dr. Ericsson points out that there are other factors involved in developing skills, factors that are neither genetic nor related to practice time. Some of these factors are: the age at which a person starts developing a skill, how isolated that person's practice is and the pressure put on that person. By providing examples of contrasting scientific views, Benedict Carey makes his argument more persuasive because in doing so he gives the impression that he is maintaining his objectivity regarding his claim. Thus, the reasoning device based on Comparison & Contrast is effectively and powerfully used to maximize the author's objectivity, and this, in turn, lends considerable support to his central idea.

Scientific examples aside, a reasoning device of direct and powerful Comparison & Contrast also helps substantiate the author's claim. Comparison & Contrast can be seen between the results of the experiment done by K. Anders Ericsson and that done by Zach Hambrick. While the study by K. Anders Ericsson indicated that practice time is the main factor influencing the development of a skill, Hambrick's later research argues that practice time only increases a person's skill by 20 to 25 percent, much less when in an academic environment. Hambrick claims "practice time is not as important as many people have been saying." Even though Hambrick denies the claim that practice time is the main factor influencing the development of a skill, he nevertheless agrees that practice time is important and is absolutely necessary to achieve mastery. The only contrast is that K. Anders Ericsson focuses on the time sent practicing, whereas Zach Hambrick focuses more on inborn gifts, in other words, native talent. Benedict Carey presents a comparison and contrast of the results of research, but the way he presents it emphasizes his claim because his presentation clearly indicates that during the development of certain skills, it is not evident whether practice time or native talent is the most important factor. In fact, the author describes a number of scientific experiments in two dimensions: diversity and Comparison & Contrast.

This is a very efficient and effective way of using examples both to convey the author's objectivity and to show that the author knows what he is talking about

Benedict Carey projects uncertainty about which might be the decisive factor in the development of certain skills — native talent or practice time. Without the use of scientific examples and direct and powerful comparison and contrast, he would have had a hard time conveying his point of view.

NEW S A T

E S S A Y

PREP

S A T

E S S A Y

PREP

READING 4

N E W S A T
E S S A Y
P R E P
S A T
E S S A Y
P R E P
N E W S A T
E S S A Y
P R E P
S A T
E S S A Y
P R E P
N E W S A T
E S S A Y
P R E P
S A T
E S S A Y
P R E P
N E W S A T
E S S A Y
P R E P
S A T
E S S A Y
P R E P
N E W S A T
E S S A Y
P R E P

Sample Essay **13**

Student Nucleus
예비12, 2017 계관웅어학원 SAT advanced반

Eric Schmidt and Jared Cohen argues that the electronic age compels people to exercise extreme vigilance in order to maintain their privacy in the future. Eric Schmidt and Jared Cohen use diverse examples and effective reasoning based on clear cause and effect.

Through the argumentative technique of diverse examples, the passage author promotes a thesis regarding. Eric Schmidt and Jared Cohen provide examples on the private information that can be exposed to the public. Every email sent from the president's BlackBerry is recorded permanently and the public can access them under the Presidential Records Act. Not only the president, but anyone's information can be shared easily. Anything one says and writes, the website one visits, the people one include in his/her online network, what one "liked" and even what others who are connected to one do and say can be exposed. Furthermore, these information stays permanently. Even though one clicks on the delete button, the data is rarely erased on computers: operating systems tend to remove only a file's listing from internal directory. As Eric Schmidt and Jared Cohen give examples, they strengthen the argument, because the readers are told about the possible damage they could face and are alerted of the potential danger. The reader would realize how important it is to protect their privacy. In addition, they would agree that using effective tools provided by companies for security and privacy are necessary, leading them to use these tools.

Diverse examples aside, the argumentative technique of clear cause and effect also substantiates Eric Schmidt and Jared Cohen's claim. The cause that every information nowadays are being stored as a near-permanent data, and without utilizing tools for security and privacy there is a high risk of one's information to be hacked or exposed to the public. Therefore, using effective tools maximize the control of one's privacy and security. An example of a tool is a cloud-based storage, which adds another layer of protection for users and their information. Also, these tools have a high chance of being used in the future. As the multilayer backup system will make online interactions more efficient and productive as well as reducing the risk of being hacked. Because Eric Schmidt and Jared Cohen used cause and effect, it conveys the importance of utilizing tools functioning of protection. It makes the reason logical why readers would have to use these tools, not just because of the risk of being hacked but also the potential benefits these tools have that will be used in the future.

Eric Schmidt and Jared Cohen emphasizes the danger the readers might face without the use of effective tools to protect one's privacy and security. Also, they argue that utilizing these tools are necessary because it would have an affect on the future. Without the use of these devices, Eric Schmidt and Jared Cohen would have had trouble conveying their argument.

Problem 1:

Even though this student started well by identifying Cause & Effect in the introduction, ignoring both fine Comparison & Contrast and Irony was a major oversight; both of these are particularly outstanding elements in the passage and need to be identified and dealt with.

Problem 2:

Student Nucleus mentions "argumentative technique" in the second paragraph, but providing diverse examples is not an argumentative technique. Additionally, it is not at all clear what this student is trying to achieve when he or she mentions a specific example used by the author; the point student Nucleus is trying to make is obviously related to Diversity.

Problem 3:

The discussion of Cause & Effect is dealt with a little bit better than is that of examples, but even this gets progressively more digressive. The Cause and Effect should have been identified independently and the possible strong correlation should have been fully discussed. Student Nucleus manages to accomplish about half this.

Eric Schmidt and Jared Cohen argues that the electronic age compels ^people to exercise extreme vigilance in order to maintain their privacy in the future. Eric Schmidt and Jared Cohen use diverse examples and effective reasoning based on clear cause and effect. → + comparison & contrast + irony

point being?

Through the argumentative technique of diverse examples, the passage author promotes a thesis (regarding) Eric Schmidt and Jared Cohen provide examples on the private information that can be exposed to the public. Every email sent from the president's BlackBerry is recorded permanently and the public can access them under the Presidential Records Act. Not only the president, but anyone's information can be shared easily. Anything one says and writes, the website one visits, the people one include in his/her online network, what one "liked" and even what others who are connected to one do and say can be exposed. Furthermore, these information stays permanently. Even though, one clicks on the delete button, the data is rarely erased on computers; operating systems tend to remove only a file's listing from internal directory. As Eric Schmidt and Jared Cohen give examples, they strengthen the argument, because the readers are told about the possible damage they could face and are alerted of the potential danger; the reader would realize how important it is to protect their privacy. In addition, they would agree that using effective tools provided by companies for security and privacy are necessary, leading them to use these tools.

Diverse examples (aside), the argumentative technique of clear cause and effect also substantiates Eric Schmidt and Jared Cohen's claim. The cause that every information nowadays are being stored as a near-permanent data, and without utilizing tools for security and privacy there is a high risk of one's information to be hacked ~~one or~~ exposed to the public. Therefore, using effective tools maximize the control of one's privacy and security. An example of a tool is a cloud-based storage, which adds another layer of protection for users and their information. Also, these tools have a high chance of being used in the future As the multilayer backup system will make online interactions more efficient and productive as well as reducing the risk of being hacked Because Eric Schmidt and Jared Cohen used cause and effect, it conveys the importance of utilizing tools functioning of protection. It makes the reason logical why readers would have to use ~~this~~ these tools, not just because of the risk of being hacked but also the potential benefits these tools have that will be used in the future.

Eric Schmidt and Jared Cohen emphasizes the danger the readers might face without the use of effective tools ~~If~~ to protect one's privacy and security. Also, they argue that ~~these~~ utilizing these tools are necessary because it would have an affect on the future. Without the use of these devices, Eric Schmidt and Jared Cohen would have had trouble conveying their argument

1. You missed two outstanding elements that are used in the reading.
2. Many of your arguments are ~~s~~ not really based on the reading
3. Constantly used odd structures.

$3/2/2.5 = 7.5 \times 2 = 15/2x$

Sample Essay 14

Student Electronic Cloud
예비11, 2017 계관웅어학원 SAT advanced반

Eric Schmidt and Jared Cohen build an argument to convince their audience that the electronic age compels us to exercise extreme vigilance in order to maintain our privacy in the future. They utilize irony, reasoning based on cause and effect and diverse examples to create a compelling argument.

Firstly, Schmidt and Cohen initiate their argument addressing the problems that lead to insecurity such as our reliance on cloud-based storage. Then, they shows irony that the mechanisms that were invented "to save us from our own carelessness" actually lead us to difficulty maintaining our privacy. They used irony to make a point to the audience that the mechanisms that were created for our benefits actually give negative effects. The use of irony makes the audience to be aware of the device they use in their daily life.

Moreover, Schmidt and Cohen state the cause and effect of the usage of the systems and devices. As aforementioned, it was created "to save us from our own carelessness" and furthermore to store data. However, the effects they mentioned are mostly negative effects. There are "loss of privacy and security", "'data remanence'", and "potential for someone else to access, share or manipulate parts of our data". These effects are mentioned to make the audience be aware of the danger they might be situated in. The effects caution the audience to not carelessly use their devices and systems. The audience would take action and exercise vigilance which was what Schmidt and Cohen are arguing for. No audience would like their personal things to be exposed to everyone, so the mentioning of these negative effects encourages the audience to maintain security for themselves.

Lastly, Schmidt and Cohen give an example. They mention today's president and state that today's president's all record are saved and accessible to the public. By showing that that the president is no exceptional, Schmidt and Cohen emphasize to the audience that everyone has insecure privacy, and no one is an exception. The audience would know that they are part of the "everyone", so they would work to maintain their privacy and increase awareness.

To sum up, Schmidt and Cohen elaborately make an argument to persuade the audience that the electronic age compels us to exercise extreme vigilance to maintain privacy in the future. To strengthen the logic and persuasiveness of their argument, they utilize irony, reasoning based on cause and effect, and diverse examples. They made the audience to be cautious and consider about the problems when they use their devices and systems.

Plus:

In the introduction student Electronic Cloud has properly identified two out of the three most outstanding rhetorical devices used by the author. I am very happy to see that.

Problem 1:

Even though most of the outstanding rhetorical devices were correctly identified in the introduction, this student seems to be unclear about why these devices are effective and puts them all together in a very unclear fashion at the beginning of the second paragraph. Student Electronic Cloud started out discussing Cause & Effect, but before the cause and the effect had been separately identified, he or she suddenly began talking about the Irony used in the passage. Unless there is a good reason for explaining them all simultaneously, this approach is obviously an ineffective and confusing way of dealing with rhetorical devices. And in this case there seems to be no reason for doing it this way.

Problem 2:

Why is it important to show that there can never be exceptions? These days there are so many computer experts, especially among the younger generation. Always bear in mind that in almost any situation you can imagine there are going to be exceptions to the rule.

Eric Schmidt and Jared Cohen build an argument to convince their audience that the electronic age compels us to exercise extreme vigilance in order to maintain our privacy in the future. They utilize Irony, reasoning based on cause and effect and diverse examples to create a compelling argument.

Firstly Schmidt and Cohen initiate their argument addressing THIS IS NOT ~~a~~ a proper assessment the problems that lead to insecurity such as our reliance on Cloud-based storage. Then, they show Irony that the mechanisms that were invented to save us from our own "carelessness" actually lead us to difficulty maintaining our privacy. They used Irony to make a point *to the audience* √ that the mechanisms that were created for our benefits actually give negative effects. The use of Irony makes the audience to be aware of the device they use in their daily life.

Moreover, Schmidt and Cohen state the cause and effect of the usage of the systems and devices. As aforementioned, it was created "to save us from our own carelessness" and furthermore to store data. However, the effects they mentioned are mostly negative effects. There are "loss of privacy and security", "data remanence", and "potential for someone else to access, share or manipulate parts of our data". These effects are mentioned to make the audience be aware of the danger they might be situated in. The effects caution the audience to not carelessly use their devices and systems. The audience would take action and exercise vigilance which was what Schmidt and Cohen are arguing for. No audience would like their personal things to be exposed to everyone, so the mentioning of these negative effects encourages the audience to maintain security for themselves.

Lastly, Schmidt and Cohen give an example. They mention today's president and state that today's president's all records are saved and accessible to the public. By showing that that the president is no exceptional, Schmidt and Cohen emphasize to the audience that everyone has insecure privacy, and noone is an exception. The audience would know that they are part of the "everyone", so they would work to maintain their privacy and

Increase awareness.

To sum up, Schmidt and Cohen elaborately make an argument to persuade the audience that the electronic age compels us to exercise extreme vigilance to maintain privacy in the future. To strengthen the logic and persuasiveness of their argument, they utilize Irony, reasoning based on cause and effect, and diverse examples. They made the audience to be cautious when they use their devices and systems. And consider about the problems

1. Read very carefully the comment on irony; eventhough irony is definately there, the way you talked about is very odd.

2. In general, this is a decent and properly written analysis.

$4/2.5/4 = 10.5 \times 2$
$= 21/24$

Sample Essay 15

Student Great Barrier Reef
고2, 2017 계관웅어학원 SAT advanced반

Most people are aware of the fact that there are several advantages as a result of advanced technology. Nonetheless, it is also an unrefutable fact that some disadvantages follow as well. In the passage, Eric Schmidt and Jared Cohen build an argument to persuade their audience that the electronic age compels us to exercise extreme vigilance in order to maintain our privacy in the future through the use of effective reasoning and rhetorical appeals.

To begin with, Schmidt and Cohen underpins the fact that every information will be recorded by using effective reasoning. They demonstrate that nowadays, when one uploads any notes or photos, or share any documents, it will all be recorded, by writing, "Data is rarely erased on computers; operating systems tend to remove only a file's listing from the internal directory …" The authors make the readers realize how their everyday routines can be or could have been recorded through the use of advanced technology. By doing so, they successfully urge their audience to be aware of the fact that anything they upload in any kind of social media will not be deleted, although they think they "deleted".

Moreover, Schmidt and Cohen uses rhetorical appeals in order to reach to their audience to convey their message that be careful of your uploads since your privacy can be threatened in the future just because of your single writing on your facebook, blog and more. The authors maximize the effect of persuasion by using pronoun 'you' and abreviation. For instance, they effectively warn their audience to think once more before the audience upload something on social media, as if they are friends of their audience, by writing, "Since information wants to be free, don't write anything down you don't want read back to you in court or printed on the front page of a newspaper, as the saying goes." Furthermore, by using abreviation, such as "don't", the authors make their audience feel like if they are friends to each other, advising. Overall, the authors effectively are rhetorical appeals like choice of a pronoun and abreviation in order to help their audience realize that they should be careful about their activities online since those activities can threaten their privacy.

In conclusion, Eric Schmdit and Jared Cohen successfully warns their audience to be careful about their online activities in social media since they can threaten their privacy. The author build their argument that the electronice(?) age leads us to exercise extreme vigilance in order to maintain our privacy in the future more persuasive through the use of effective reasoning and rhetorical devices, leading their audience to think about possible acts to protect their privacy.

Problem 1:

There are two critical errors in the introduction. First, the student failed to identify any rhetorical devices used by the author. Second, "effective reasoning" is part of "rhetorical appeal".

Problem 2:

At the very beginning of the second paragraph student Great Barrier Reef uses an awkward sentence; "… every information will be recorded by effective reasoning." This gives the impression that it is effective reasoning itself that will record the information. The student seems to have problems constructing even simple sentences and needs to spend some time and effort upgrading his or her fundamental writing skills before advancing to the challenge of rhetorical analysis.

Problem 3:

Based on what is written in the third paragraph, it is rather obvious that student Great Barrier Reef is confused about the meaning of "rhetorical appeal". Rhetorical appeal covers everything the author does to make his or her writing persuasive; this may include using diverse examples, all kinds of styles, and effective reasoning. Anybody who has any trouble understanding such fundamental terms and concepts is advised to review the early chapters of this manual.

Most people are aware of the fact that there are several advantages as a result of advanced technology. Nonetheless, it is also an unrefutable fact that some disadvantages follow as well. In the passage, Eric Schmidt and Jared Cohen build an argument to persuade their audience that the electronic age compels us to exercise extreme vigilance in order to maintain our privacy in the future through the use of effective reasoning and rhetorical appeals. Not specific enough

To begin with, Schmidt and Cohen underpins the fact that every information will be recorded by using effective reasoning. They demonstrate that nowadays, when one uploads any notes or photos, or share any documents, it will all be recorded, by writing, "Data is rarely erased on computers; operating systems tend to remove only a file's listing from the internal directory..." The authors make the readers realize how their everyday routines can be or could have been recorded through the use of advanced technology. By doing so, they successfully urge their audience to be aware of the fact that anything they upload in any kind of social media will not be deleted, although they think they "deleted".

Moreover, Schmidt and Cohen uses rhetorical appeals in order to reach to their audience to convey their message, that be careful of your uploads since your privacy can be threatened in the future just because of your single writing on your facebook, blog and more. The authors maximize the effect of persuasion by using pronoun 'you' and abreviation. For instance, they effectively warn their audience to think once more before the audience uploads something on social media, as if they are friends of their audience, by writing, "Since information wants to be free, don't write anything down you don't want read back to you in court or printed on the front page of a newspaper, as the saying goes." Furthermore, by using abreviations, such as "don't", the authors make their audience feel like if they are friends to each other, advising. Overall, the authors effectively use rhetorical appeals like choice of a pronoun and abbreviation in order to help their audience realize that they should be careful about their activities online since those activities can threaten their privacy.

In conclusion, Eric Schmidt and Jared Cohen successfully warns their audience to be careful about their online activities in social media since they can threaten their privacy. The author build their argument that the electronic age leads us to exercise extreme vigilance in order to maintain our privacy in the future more persuasive through the use of effective reasoning and rhetorical devices, leading their audience to think about possible acts to protect their privacy.

You completely ignored class instructions, which puts/ the entire essay in the risk of being not a good analysis; read them over and over again very carefully

$3/2/3 = 8 \times 2 = 16 / 2\%$

Sample Essay **16**

Student Jackal
고2, 2017 계관웅어학원 SAT advanced반

In their essay, Eric Schmidt and Jared Cohen argues that the electronic age compels us to exercise extreme vigilance in order to maintain our privacy in the future. The authors use scientific evidence and logical reasoning, especially cause & effect and comparison & contrast to build their logic. Moreover, they maintain a warning tone throughout the essay which appeals to the readers' emotion.

First of all, Schmidt and Cohen use scientific evidence. In the first paragraph, they explain in detail about how data is never deleted: "Data is rarely erased on computers; operating systems tend to remove only a file's listing from the internal directory, keeping the file's contents." This scientific evidence slightly shocks the readers (a shock for those who didn't know) by showing how any private data will remain. Because this evidence strongly relates to the reader's everyday life, it makes them empathic with the danger of the electronic age, and persuades the audience that it will need hard effort to protect our privacy in the future.

Second of all, the authors use logical reasoning methods such as cause and effect, and comparison and contrast. In the third paragraph, there is an obvious cause and effect for why people will depend on cloud storage. The cause is that people try "avoiding risks of hard-drive crashes, computer thefts or document loss": people will trust perfect machines than themselves, full of mistakes. The effect is that "people will increasingly trust cloud storage," which is easily "accessed by multiple networks and uers." By mentioning the cause of the dangerous result, the authors build persuasive logic for why in the future it will be hard to maintain privacy. Also, in paragraph 5, they compare president Nixon with today's president: "Nixon may have erased sections of audio tapes containing his conversations about the Watergate scandal, but today's president faces a permanent record of every e-mail sent from his Blackberry." By comparing the two presidents, Schmidt and Cohen compares the present to the past. Using a humorous example, the authors ironically persuades the audience that we might not be able to erase our own failures and scandals, not only the president's, in the future. This humorous and ironic comparison persuades the readers by giving a real-life example of how the paradigm changed.

Lastly, the author's warning tone appeals strongly to the readers' emotion. The authors use a second person singular pronoun, "you" which directly calls the audience: "And you cannot assume there is a simple delete button." This warning tone appeals to ethos because it implies that the authors are worried of the human species from the upcoming privacy alert, which persuades the audience by both being alerted by the danger and by making them trust the authors as good people who care for humans. The use of a second person pronoun is also important because it enables direct communication between the authors and the audience. The readers will feel like they are actually talking to the authors because they find a "you" in the essay. Overall, the alerting tone persuades the readers by appealing to direct emotional alert.

In conclusion, Schmidt and Cohen uses scientific evidence, reasoning methods such as cause and effect and comparision & contrast to persuade the audience at the intellectual level. Also, they appeal to emotion by an alerting tone and the use of a Second person pronoun. These devices build a well-balanced essay between logic and emotional appeal, making the authors' claim persuasive.

Problem 1:

In the introduction student Jackal properly identified Cause & Effect along with Comparison & Contrast. It could have been much better if the student had also identified Irony, but this is not a big problem.

Problem 2:

In the third paragraph the student mentions "ironic comparison", so it would have been very easy to include Irony in the introduction. In addition, student Jackal does not make it clear why and how "⋯ humorous and ironic comparison persuades the reader by giving a real-life example ⋯."

Problem 3:

This student uses (more than) a few awkward sentences; for example "This warning tone appeals to ethos because it implies that the authors are worried of human species from upcoming privacy alert ⋯." Just because somebody gives a warning, it does not mean that that person is worried about the entire human species. Also, the preposition "from" is wrongly used, creating a sentence that doesn't make sense.

Plus:

The discussion of Cause & Effect was generally well done as was that related to Comparison & Contrast. Both were backed up with sufficient details.

In their essay, Eric Schmidt and Jared Cohen argues that the electronic age compels us to exercise extreme vigilance in order to maintain our privacy in the future. The authors use scientific evidence and logical reasoning, especially cause & effect and comparison & contrast to build their logic. Moreover, they maintain a warning tone throughout the essay which appeals to the readers' emotion. what about irony?

First of all, Schmidt and Cohen use scientific evidence. In the first paragraph, they explain in detail about how data is never deleted: "Data is rarely erased on computers; operating systems tend to remove only a file's listing from the internal directory, keeping the file's contents." This scientific evidence slightly shocks the readers (a shock for those who didn't know) by showing how any private data will remain. Because this evidence strongly relates to the reader's everyday life, it makes them empathize with the danger of the electronic age, and persuades the audience that it will need hard effort to protect our privacy in the future.

Second of all, the authors use logical reasoning methods such as cause and effect, and comparison and contrast. In the third paragraph, there is an obvious cause and effect for why people will depend on cloud storage. The cause is that people try "avoiding risks of hard-drive crashes, computer thefts or document loss": people will trust perfect machines than themselves, full of mistakes. The effect, is that "people will increasingly trust cloud storage" which is easily "accessed by multiple networks and users." By mentioning the cause of the dangerous result, the authors build persuasive logic for why the in future it will be hard to maintain privacy. Also, in paragraph 5, they compare President Nixon with today's president: "Nixon may have erased sections of audio tapes containing his conversations about the watergate scandal, but today's president faces a permanent record of every e-mail sent from his Blackberry." By comparing the two presidents, Schmidt and Cohen compares the present to the past. Using a humorous example, the authors

Ironically persuades the audience that we might not be able to erase our own failures and scandals, not only the president's, in the future. This humorous and ironic comparison persuades the readers by giving a real-life example, of how the paradigm changed.

Lastly, the authors' warning tone appeals strongly to the readers' emotion. The authors use a second person singular pronoun, "you" which directly calls the audience: "And you cannot assume there is a simple delete button." This warning tone appeals to ethos because it implies that the authors are worried of the human species from the upcoming privacy alert, which persuades the audience by both being alerted by the danger and by making them trust the authors as good people who care for humans. The use of a second person pronoun is also important because it enables direct communication between the authors and the audience. The readers will feel like they are actually talking to the authors because they find a "you" in the essay. Overall, the alerting tone persuades the readers by appealing to direct emotional alert.

In conclusion, Schmidt and Cohen uses scientific evidence, reasoning methods such as cause and effect, and comparison & contrast to persuade the audience at the intellectual level. Also, they appeal to emotion by an alerting tone and the use of a second person pronoun. These devices build a well-balanced essay between logic and emotional appeal, making the authors' claim persuasive.

Except that you missed irony as an outstanding element, this is a decent analysis without any significant problem

4 / 3 / 4 = 11 × 2 = 22/24

An Improved Version
of Sample Essay 16
for achieving the maximum score

In their essay, Eric Schmidt and Jared Cohen argue that the electronic age compels us to exercise extreme vigilance in order to maintain our privacy, especially in the future. The authors use scientific evidence and logical reasoning, especially Cause & Effect and Comparison & Contrast to build their logic along with a literary device, Irony. Moreover, they maintain a warning tone throughout the essay, which appeals to the emotions of the reader.

First of all, Schmidt and Cohen use scientific evidence. In the first paragraph, they explain in detail how electronic data is never actually deleted: "Data is rarely erased on computers; operating systems tend to remove only a file's listing from the internal directory, keeping the file's contents." This scientific evidence draws attention to the fact that any and all electronic data, including the most private data, never cease to exist, which would certainly be shocking to a reader who did not already know this. This kind of revelation is sure to grab the attention of many readers and give the impression that the author is quite knowledgeable about this field, which in turn will increase the credibility and objectivity of the central idea. Furthermore, because electronic communication is part of most reader's everyday life, the permanence of this data will alert people to the danger of the electronic age, and will easily persuade them that they need to make a concerted effort to protect their privacy now and in the future.

Second of all, the authors use logical reasoning devices such as that based on Cause & Effect, and Comparison & Contrast. The third paragraph demonstrates that there is an obvious cause and effect relationship that will result in people being dependent on cloud storage. The cause is that people are interested in "avoiding risks of hard-drive crashes, computer thefts or document loss": people will trust machines more than they trust themselves. full of mistakes. The effect is that "people will increasingly trust cloud storage", which is easily "accessed by multiple networks and users." By establishing the inevitability of the cause and the danger of the result, the authors build persuasive logic as to why, in the future, it will be very hard for anyone to maintain privacy. Also, in paragraph 5, they compare president Nixon with today's president: "Nixon may have erased sections of audio tapes containing his conversations about the Watergate scandal, but today's president has to deal with a permanent record of every e-mail ever sent from his BlackBerry." By comparing the two presidents, Schmidt and Cohen compares the present with the past. This particular comparison is very effective because it proves two things at the same time: the way events unfolded in the past is not the way they will happen in the future, and even a powerful modern president cannot erase everything. Using a humorous example, the authors persuade us that we, ordinary people, can never escape from our failures and scandals. This rather humorous and ironic comparison is persuasive because it offers a real-life example of how the paradigm has changed.

Lastly, the author's warning tone appeals strongly to the readers' emotions. This is also very useful in conveying the central idea because authors' other rhetorical devices might be perceived as rather technical and dull. In order to avoid this, the authors use a second person perspective, "you" which directly addresses the reader: "And you cannot assume there is a simple delete button." This warning tone appeals to ethos because it implies that the authors' intention is to warn the human race about the upcoming threat to privacy, which is persuasive because the we humans are not only being alerted to the danger but are being made to trust the authors who seem to care about us. The use of a second person perspective is important also because it enables direct communication between the authors and the reader; after all, the central idea is deeply embedded in everyday life.

In conclusion, Schmidt and Cohen use scientific evidence, reasoning devices such as that of Cause & Effect and that of Comparison & Contrast to persuade the reader. Also, they appeal to emotion by using an alerting tone and by the use of a second person perspective. These devices help build a well-balanced essay that appeals to both our logic and our emotions; without one of these the entire essay would have been rather dull or one-sided.

READING 5

Sample Essay 17

Student Plasma
예비12, 2017 계관웅어학원 SAT advanced반

Throughout the passage, Peter Singer builds an argument to persuade his audience that animals feel pain. To successfully convince the audience, the author employs stylistic element of rhetorical approach, and reasoning such as comparison and contrast.

Firstly, Singer continuously makes use of stylistic element of rhetorical question to successfully build his argument. This device is continuously used throughout the extract: three in the first paragraph, one in the second paragraph, and one in the last paragraph. This is a very effective tool to persuade the audience, as it not only attracts the audience's attention, but also makes them to reflect on the matter. These questions effectively supports the central claim by stimulating the audience's curiosity.

Then, the author employs reasoning of comparison and contrast to develop his idea. Throughout paragraph three and four, the author compares mammals and birds to robots. He draws the similarity between them in that they can both move, and draws the contrast that the robot are 'artificially constructed' contrary to animals which have a 'nervous system' which 'evolved as our own (human's nerve system) did: This is a very effective reasoning which helps to strengthen the central claim as it also implies the similarity between human and animals.

To conclude, the author makes use of rhetorical question and comparison and contrast to deliver his central claim. Without these device, the author would not have been able to convince the audience with his central claim.

Problem 1:

Student Plasma made a typical and recurring error by missing one of the two most important reasoning devices: Cause & Effect. Remember again that Comparison & Contrast and Cause & Effect almost always occur together. If you find one, look for the other.

Problem 2:

A Rhetorical Question is a powerful tool but it is often used incorrectly. Whenever we discuss this particular device, we need to explain why it is effective in conveying the central idea or the thesis. This student failed to do just that.

Problem 3:

Even though Comparison & Contrast was very effectively assessed, the Comparison & Contrast between different animal species was not the point; it is the Comparison & Contrast between animals and humans that needs to be addressed in order to show the strength of the author's argument.

NAME: Class: Adv.

Throughout the passage, Peter Singer builds an argument to persuade his audience that animals feel pain. To successfully convince the audience, the author employs stylistic element of rhetorical approach, and reasoning such as comparison and contrast. + cause & effect

question

Firstly, Singer continuously makes use of stylistic element of rhetorical question to successfully build his argument. This device is continuously used throughout the excerpt: three in the first paragraph, one in the second paragraph, and one in the last paragraph. This is a very effective tool to persuade the audience, as it not only attracts the audience's attention, but also makes them to reflect on the matter. These questions effectively supports the central claim by stimulating the audience's curiosity. why effective? ✓

Then, the author employs reasoning of comparison and contrast to develop his idea. Throughout paragraph three and four, the author compares mammals and birds to robots. He draws the similarity between them in that they can both move, and draws the contrast that the robot are 'artificially constructed' contrary to animals which have a 'nervous system' which 'evolved as our own (human's nerve system) did'. This is a very effective reasoning which helps to strengthen the central claim as it also implies the similarity between human and animals.

→ This TS only a summary.

To conclude, the author makes use of rhetorical question and comparison and contrast to deliver his central claim. Without these devices, the author would not have been able to convince the audience with his central claim.

You failed to identify one outstanding element; cause & effect, and this is a significant problem, because it is among the most essential devices that the author used throughout the passage

$$4/2.5/4 = 10.5 \times 2 = 21/24$$

Sample Essay 18

Student Peregrine
예비12, 2017 계관웅어학원 SAT advanced반

The author, Peter Singer builds an argument to persuade his audience that there are no good reasons, scientific or philosophic, for denying that animal feel pain. The author utilize logical reasoning based on comparison and contrast and use cause and effect as the evidence to give strength to the reasonings.

In third, fourth, and ninth paragraphs the author uses comparison and contrast to prove that there are no ways to deny that animal cannot feel pain. "Nearly all the evterral signs that lead us to infer pain in other humans can be seen in other species, especially the species most closely related to us — mammals and birds." This comparison of body structure between human and mammals and birds is effective in strengthening the author's central idea as it makes the audience think that logically, if mammals and birds are most closely related to human they should also feel the pain because human feel the pain. Morevoer author uses contrast, "it is surely unreasonable to suppose that nervous systems that are virtually identical physiologically, have a common origin and a common evolutionary function, and result in similar forms of behavior in similar circumstances should actually operate in an entirely different manner on the level of subjective feelings." This contrast between two contradictory claim effectively makes his argument stronger because the author previously explain that similar nervous system in other species like mammals and birds make them to feel similar pain as human. The author uses another contrast in the second last paragraph. The author mentions one philosopher's idea that go against the author's main argument "we cannot meaningfully attribute states of consciousness to being without language." The author uses this philosopher's idea to strengthen his idea by proving that the philosopher's idea is wrong in the following sentences.

Additionally, the author uses cause and effect as the evidence of the comparison and contrasts that one mentioned in previous paragraph to back up his main idea. In third paragraph, the author says "these animals [mammals and birds] have nervous systems very like ours, which respond physicologically like ours do to painful stimuli: an initial rise of blood pressure, dilated pupils." The author use this to explain that due to this cause that having similar nervous system, the effect logically follows : Those animals feel pain. The author uses another cause and effect to explain that "interests and activities of animals are correlated with awareness and feeling in the same way as my [human] own." The author says "A capacity to feel pain obviously enhances a species' prospects for survival, since it causes members of the species to avoid sources of injury." This makes the author's point clear that the cause which is pain make animals to avoid from getting an injury and this effect is from animals' awareness and feelings.

The author uses comparison and contrast to strengthen his idea and uses cause and effect as an evidence to back up his claim that animals feel pain and it cannot be denied.

Problem 1:

Student Peregrine clearly identified the two most important reasoning devices: Cause & Effect and Comparison & Contrast, but failed to mention Rhetorical Question. In this case, completely ignoring Rhetorical Question is a rather significant oversight because the given reading started off with *four* Rhetorical Questions.

Problem 2:

In the second paragraph this student correctly identified the comparison and the contrast and also correctly explained why this Comparison & Contrast was effective in conveying the central idea. However, the explanation could have been and should have been more elaborate. Student Peregrine should have explained that the reason that animals feel pain the same way humans do is that their anatomy is similar to that of humans. Do not take anything for granted; the more detailed and elaborate the explanation is, the better it is. There are no exceptions to this rule.

Problem 3:

It is admirable that student Peregrine has tried to show the connection between Cause & Effect and Comparison & Contrast, but there is a problem with how he or she attempted to do this. The student should not have said "the author uses cause and effect as the evidence of comparison[s] and contrasts ⋯." In the given passage, the author showed Cause & Effect by utilizing Comparison & Contrast, but

Cause & Effect cannot be referred to as evidence but rather as a way of showing why this Comparison & Contrast was important in the process of conveying the central idea.

Week 10-1 EW	NAME:	Class: *adv*

The author, Peter Singer builds an argument to persuade his audience that there are no good reasons, scientific or philosophical, for denying that animal feel pain. The author utilize logical reasoning based on comparison and contrast and use a cause and effect as the evidence to give strength to the reasoning.

+ rhetorical question + Any other rhetorical devices ?

In third, fourth, and ninth paragraphs the author uses comparison and contrast to prove that there are no ways to deny that animal cannot feel pain. "Nearly
can(?)
all the external signs that lead us to infer pain in other humans can be seen in other species, especially the species most closely related to us — mammals and birds". This comparison of body structure between human and mammals and birds is effective in strengthening the author's central idea as it makes the audience think that logically, if mammals and birds are most closely related to human, they should also feel the pain because human feel the pain. Moreover author uses contrast, "It is surely unreasonable to suppose that nervous systems that are virtually identical physiologically, have a common origin and a common evolutionary function, and result in similar forms of behavior in similar circumstances should actually operate in an entirely different manner on the level of subjective feelings." This contrast between two contradictory claim effectively makes his argument stronger because the author previously explain that similar nervous system in other spieces like mammals and birds make them to feel similar pain as human. The author uses another contrast in the second last paragraph. The author mentions one philosopher's idea that go against the author's main argument "we cannot meaningfully attribute states of consciousness to being without language." The author uses this philosopher's idea to strengthen his idea by proving that the philosopher's idea is wrong in the following sentences.

Additionally, the author uses cause and effect as the evidence of the comparison and contrasts that are mentioned in previous paragraph to back up his main idea. In third paragraph, the author says "these animals [mammals and birds] have nervous systems very like ours, which respond physiologically like ours do to painful stimuli: an initial rise of blood pressure, dilated pupils..." The author use this to explain that due to this cause, that having similar nervous system, the effect logically follows: Those animals feel pain. The author uses another cause and effect to explain that "interests and activities of animals are correlated with awareness and feeling in the same way as my [human] own" The author says "A capacity to feel pain obviously enhances a species' prospects for survival, since it causes members of the species to avoid sources of injury." This makes the author's point clear that the cause which is pain make animals to avoid from getting an injury and this effect is from animals' awareness and feelings.

The author uses comparison and contrast to strengthen his idea and uses cause and effect as an evidence to back up his claim that animals feel pain and it cannot be denied

1. Try to come up with at least two rhetorical devices; cause & effect and comparison & contrast are fall into the same category of rhetorical device: reasoning device; other examples would be diverse examples and/or effective styles such as strong diction or literary devices.

2.

Sample Essay 19

Student Mitochondrias
고2, 2017 계관웅어학원 SAT advanced반

The author, Peter Singer, tries to persuade his audience that animals feel pain, just as humans do. He utilizes several devices to strengthen his central idea, which are authoritative evidence, effective reasoning based on comparison and contrast, and rhetorical questions.

In the fifth paragraph, the author quotes the words of "Lord Brain, one of the most eminent neurologists of our (author's) time." The following is a part of what Lord Brain had said. " I personally set no reason for conceding mind to my fellow men and denying it to animals. I at least cannot doubt that the interests and activities of animals are correlated with awareness and feeling in the same way a my own." That "one of the most eminent neurologist" had argued for the same position as the author effectively strengthens the author's central idea. Being a neurologist itself contributes to the central idea as it shows that he is an expert on pain, but his fame further illustrates the point because it means that he is an experienced expert. Moreover, by utilizing quote by Lord Brain, the author is able to make his main argument more solid. Due to the central idea's subjective nature, this passage might have been dull and unpersuasive, but this piece of authoritative evidence resolves this problem and further adds power to the central idea.

Additionally, the author compares pain in humans and other species, mainly mammals and birds, in the third paragraph. "The behavioral signs include loathing, facial contortions, moaning, yelping or other forms of calling …. In addition, we know that these animals have nervous systems very like ours, which respond physiologically like ours do to painful stimuli : an initial rise of blood pressure, dilated pupils, an increased pulse rate …" By associating the nervous system of humans and mammals, the author is able to prove that the similar structures of nervous systems will lead to the conclusion that both species are susceptible to pain. This directly supports the author's central idea that animals can feel pain as well. With this simple comparison, the author can easily persuade his audience of his main argument.

Finally, in the last paragraph, the author uses a rhetorical question to prove that the thought "language is necessary in evaluating whether pain can be felt in animals" is implausible. Disproving this notion is crucial as it disagrees with the author's central idea. "Human infants and young children are unable to use language. Are we to deny that a year-old child can suffer?" This rhetorical question effectively conveys the idea that language is not important when indging(?) for pain as it appeals to common sense. Whether babies feel pain is not, and has never been subject to question; asking the possibility of denying this point, therefore, is equivalent to directly challenging the claim that language is a necessary factor in deciding the ability to feel pain. As a result, through this rhetorical question, the author is able to contribute to his central idea.

With these three devices — authoritative evidence, comparison and contrast, and rhetorical questions —, the author is able to add much power to his central idea. The audience could probably get convinced that animals feel pain, just like humans, after reading this passage.

Problem 1:

In the introduction student Mitochondrias failed to mention one of four outstanding rhetorical devices used by the author: Cause & Effect. Fortunately, the other three have been properly identified.

Problem 2:

Proving is not the same as arguing. In the fourth paragraph student Mitochondrias argues that the Rhetorical Questions used by the author "proved" something, but no Rhetorical Question can prove anything. Rhetorical Questions are used to *emphasize* a point or advance an *argument*. Am I correct? The Rhetorical Questions used in the given reading are no exception.

Plus 1:

Almost all the outstanding rhetorical devices are properly identified.

Plus 2:

The discussion of Comparison & Contrast is to-the-point and precise.

The author, Peter Singer, tries to persuade his audience that animals feel pain, just as humans do. He utilizes several devices to strengthen his central idea, which are authoritative evidence, effective reasoning based on comparison and contrast, and rhetorical questions. + cause & effect
+ ~~rhetorical question~~ Srry

In the fifth paragraph, the author quotes the words of "Lord Brain, one of the most eminent neurologists of our (author's) time". The following is a part of what Lord Brain had said." I personally see no reason for conceding mind to my fellow men and denying it to animals. I at least cannot doubt that the interests and activities of animals are correlated with awareness and feeling in the same way as my own." That "one of the most eminent neurologist" had argued for the same position as the author effectively strengthens the author's central idea. Being a neurologist itself contributes to the central idea as it shows that he is an expert on pain, but his fame further illustrates the point because it means that he is an 'experienced' expert. Moreover, by utilizing a quote by Lord Brain, the author is able to make his main argument more solid. Due to the central idea's subjective nature, this passage might have been dull and unpersuasive, but this piece of authoritative evidence resolves this problem and further adds power to the central idea.

Additionally, the author compares pain in humans and other species, mainly mammals and birds, in the third paragraph. "The behavioral signs include writhing, facial contortions, moaning, yelping or other forms of calling... In addition, we know that these animals have nervous systems very like ours, which respond physiologically like ours do to painful stimuli: an initial rise of blood pressure, dilated pupils, an increased pulse rate..." By associating the nervous systems of humans and mammals, the author is able to prove that the similar structures of nervous systems will lead to the conclusion that both species are susceptible to pain. This directly supports the author's central idea that animals can feel pain as well. With this simple comparison, the author can easily persuade his audience of his main argument.

Finally, in the last paragraph, the author uses a rhetorical question the thought,

to prove that "language is necessary in evaluating whether pain can be felt in animals. Disproving this notion is crucial, as it disagrees with the author's central idea. "Human infants and young children are unable to use language. Are we to deny that a year-old child can suffer?" This rhetorical question effectively conveys the idea that language is not important when judging for pain as it appeals to common sense. Whether babies feel pain is not, and has never been subject to question; asking the possibility of denying this point, therefore, is equivalent to directly challenging the claim that language is a necessary factor in deciding the ability to feel pain. As a result, through this rhetorical question, the author is able to contribute to his central idea.

With these three devices — authoritative evidence, comparison and contrast, and rhetorical questions —, the author is able to add much power to his central idea. The audience would probably get convinced that the animals feel pain, just like humans, after reading this passage.

1. precise
2. to-the-point approach
3. good organization

$4/3/4 = 11 \times 2 = 22/24$

Sample Essay 20

Student Entropy
예비10, 2017 계관웅어학원 SAT advanced반

Drunk in our sense of superiority over other animals, we seem to be acknowledging that humans are the only animals that can feel pain. That at least, is what singer, the author of the passage, has in perspective while addressing the issue. In order to persuade the majority on his belief that animals feel pain, Singer uses a brilliant combination of cause & effect, comparison & contrast, as well as supportive evidence.

Cause and effect plays a key role in singer's passage to address the common misperception regarding the topic and to show the resulting consequences that affect our thoughts. Singer describes the cause of certain misbeliefs in paragraph 1 when he throws a series of debatable questions: "Do animals other than humans feel pain?" and "Well, how do we know if anyone, human or nonhuman, feels pain?" A repetition of these questions gets the reader to start reflecting upon what they originally believed, and question the validity of supporting thoughts, if there are any. By getting the reader to have softer thoughts about their own belief, Singer can manipulate these thoughts easily in order to persuade the audience into his point of view. The effect portion does its job when Singer directly addresses the reader with the misperception effects that the 'cause' brought. Singer states in paragraph 1: "We cannot directly experience anyone else's pain" and "We can only infer that others are feeling it." These questions now describeand make the reader reform their beliefs if they were against the idea that animals feel pain, and if they were for the idea, it amplifies their supporting beliefs because Singer shows them that he is indeed on the same side as them.

Comparison & contrast is another main element in Signer's piece because it shows how really much of a difference there can be betweens humans and animals, such that even primitive senses like pain only evolved in humans. Singer starts off his main arguments with a very large comparison element: the fact that both humans and animals are mammals. Singer states in paragraph 3 that "we know that these animals have nervous system like ours." In paragraph 4, Singer also says "The nervous systems of other animals evolved as our own did" and "The evolutionary history of human beings and other animals, did not diverge until the central features of our nervous systems were already in existence." These quotations show the constant repetitions of the idea that humans are also animals. The statement especially about how our 'evolutionary divergence is not enormous' strives to correct the thought that we are immersed in; the tact that our intellectual capabilities make such a difference that we don't even consider ourself as part of nature anymore. With the comparison, Singer effectively showed the audience that we are in fact animals too, and broke the common misconception that we are not to claim that the 'pain' we feel is also present inside other animals. Now, as a contrasting example, Singer brings in robots to show the audience of something that we can believe we are completely not related to. Paragraph 4 gives an example of an artificially constructed example as a robot, which drastically contrasts from animals, because we perceive robots as the actual emotionless beings. The contrast between animals and robots are just too large that the reader is persuaded to the thought that they shouldn't perceive animals as emotionless because emotionlessness is for robots. By using comparison & contrast effectively, Singer corrects the thought of animals being emotionless, and persuades the audience to believe that animals have emotions, and they would thereby feel pain.

Last but not least, Singer brings in evidence from accredited sources to elaborate on his arguments. By introducing Lord Brain as a very prominent figure, Singer adds credibility to his argument by showing that his arguments are supported by Lord Brain himself. The second piece of evidence Singer uses is an excerpt from a book about pain. The main values does not come from the fact that this source is a book, but instead it plays a big role in summarizing Singer's arguments. "To Say that they feel less because they are lower animals is an absurdity" and "Their nervous systems are almost identical to ours" are statements that perfectly summarize the author's point of view as well as all the arguments he made in the previous paragraphs. A reminder of this sort that summarizes Singer's points in concise words serve to directly hammer in the ideas that Singer has implied throughout the passage.

In conclusion, Singer used cause & effect, comparison & contrast and supportive evidence to pursued the reader to believe that animals in foot, feel pain. These three elements combined together served to break the common misconception, address the sensible right idea and give a summarized idea for the reader to take-home with them.

Problem 1:

In this essay we see the exact same error we encountered in Sample Essay 18: the student failed to identify the Rhetorical Question while identifying the two other most important reasoning devices: Cause & Effect and Comparison & Contrast.

Problem 2:

In the second paragraph student Entropy made a mistake of combining Cause & Effect and Rhetorical Question. First of all, the reason for the combining is unclear. Second, the combination makes the flow of the analysis very hard to follow.

Problem 3:

In the beginning of the third paragraph student Entropy argues, "… a very large comparison element: the fact that both humans and animals are mammals …." Maybe the student read the passage wrong or maybe he or she is just incredibly unfamiliar with biology; in either case, this kind of basic factual error will not go unnoticed by the evaluator. Every mammal is an animal, but not every animal is a mammal. Obviously the author of the reading being analyzed did not state or even imply such nonsense.

Drunk in our sense of superiority over other animals, we seem to be acknowledging that humans are the only animals that can feel pain. That, at least, is what Singer, the author of the passage, has in perspective while addressing the issue. In order to persuade the majority on his belief that animals feel pain, Singer uses a brilliant combination of cause & effect, comparison & contrast, as well as supportive evidence. *+ rhetorical question*

Not specific enough

Cause and effect plays a key role in Singer's passage to address the common misperception regarding the topic and to show the resulting consequences that affect our thoughts. Singer describes the cause of certain misbeliefs in Paragraph 1 when he throws a series of debatable questions: "Do animals other than humans feel pain?" and "Well, how do we know if anyone, human or nonhuman, feels pain?" A repetition of these questions gets the reader to start reflecting upon what they originally believed, and question the validity of supporting thoughts, if there are any. By getting the reader to have softer thoughts about their own belief, Singer can manipulate these thoughts easily in order to persuade the audience into his point of view. The effect portion does its job when Singer directly addresses the reader with the misperception effects that the 'cause' brought. Singer states in Paragraph 1: "We cannot directly experience anyone else's pain" and "We can only infer that others are feeling it." These questions now describe and make the reader reform their beliefs if they were against the idea that animals feel pain, and if they were for the idea, it amplifies their supporting beliefs because Singer shows them that he is indeed on the same side as them.

Comparison & contrast is another main element in Singer's piece because it shows how really much of a difference there can be betweens humans and animals, such that even primitive senses like pain only evolved in humans. Singer starts off his main arguments with a very large comparison element: the fact that both humans and animals are mammals. Singer states in Paragraph 3 that "we know that these animals have nervous system like ours." In Paragraph 4, Singer also says "The nervous systems of other animals evolved as our own did" and "The evolutionary history of human beings and other animals, did not diverge until the central features of our nervous systems were already in existence." These quotations show the constant repetition of the idea that humans are also animals. The statement especially about how our 'evolutionary divergence is not enormous' strives to correct the thought that 'we are immersed in; The fact that our intellectual capabilities make such a difference that we don't even consider ourself as part of nature anymore. With the comparison, Singer effectively showed the audience that we are in fact animals too, and broke the common misconception that we are not to claim that the 'pain' we feel is also present inside other animals. Now, as a contrasting example, Singer brings in robots to show the audience of something that we can believe we are completely not related to. Paragraph 4 gives an example of an artificially contructed example as a robot, which drastically contrasts from animals, because we percieve robots as the actual emotionless beings. The contrast between animals and robots are just too large that the reader is persuaded to the thought that they shouldn't percieve animals as emotionless because emotionlessness is for robots. By using comparison & contrast effectively, Singer corrects the thought of animals being emotionless, and persuades the audience to believe that animals have emotions, and they would thereby feel pain.

Last but not least, Singer brings in evidence from accredited sources to elaborate on his arguments. By introducing Lord Brain as a very prominent figure, Singer adds credibility to his argument by showing that his arguments are supported by Lord Brain himself. The second piece of evidence Singer uses is an excerpt from a book about pain. The main value does not come from the fact that this source is a book, but instead it plays a big role in summarizing Singer's arguments. "To say that they feel less because they are lower animals is an absurdity" and "Their nervous systems are almost identical to ours" are statements that perfectly summarize the author's point of view as well as all the arguments he made in the previous paragraphs. A reminder of this sort that summarizes Singer's points in concise words serve to directly hammer in the ideas that Singer has implied throughout the passage. ← No identification of the author's devices?

In conclusion, Singer used cause&effect, comparison &contrast and supportive evidence to persuade the reader to believe that animals in fact, feel pain. These three elements combined together served to break the common misperception, address the sensible right idea and give a summarized idea for the reader to take-home with them.

Way too short
Not finished
N/A

NEW SAT
ESSAY
PREP
SAT
ESSAY
PREP

An Improved Version
of Sample Essay 20
for achieving the maximum score

"Drunk in our sense of superiority over other animals, we seem to be acknowledging that humans are the only animals that can feel pain." At least, that is the perspective on the issue offered by Singer, the author of the passage. In order to persuade the reader of his belief that animals feel pain, Singer uses a brilliant combination of Cause & Effect and Comparison & Contrast, as well as supportive evidence. In order to provoke the readers into thinking, or doubting their possible prejudice, the author began the passage with a series of rhetorical questions.

Cause & Effect plays a key role in Singer's attempt to address the common misperception regarding the topic and to show the consequences that result from this misperception. Singer describes the cause of certain erroneous beliefs in paragraph 1 when he throws out a series of debatable and seemingly rhetorical questions: "Do animals other than humans feel pain?" and "Well, how do we know if anyone, human or nonhuman, feels pain?" A repetition of these questions causes readers to start reflecting upon what they believe, and question the validity of the concepts, if any, that support this belief. By weakening the readers' thoughts about their own beliefs, Singer carefully manipulates these thoughts in order to bring the reader closer to his point of view. When Singer directly confronts the reader with the effects caused by their misperception, those effects make an impact that the reader might not soon forget. Singer states in paragraph 1: "We cannot directly experience anyone else's pain" and "We can only infer that others are feeling it." These statements can now cause the readers to doubt their prejudice, and this doubt helps amplify the central idea because people who are unsure of themselves are more open to new ideas.

Comparison & Contrast is another main element in Signer's argument because it shows that there cannot be much difference between humans and animals, and that primitive senses like pain could not have evolved only in humans. Singer starts off his main arguments with a hugely significant comparison element: the fact that humans are animals. In paragraph 3, Singer states that "we know that these animals have nervous system like ours." In paragraph 4, he also says "The nervous systems of other animals evolved as our own did," and "The evolutionary history of human beings and other animals, did not diverge until the central features of our nervous systems were already in existence." These statements are a constant repetition of the idea that humans are also animals. The statement about how our 'evolutionary divergence is not enormous' is specifically intended to correct the misconception at the heart of the matter; the idea that our intellectual capabilities make us so different that we no longer consider ourselves as part of nature. With this comparison, Singer effectively proves that the difference between animals and us is not great, and shattered the common misconception that animals don't feel pain. As a contrasting example, Singer then brings up robots in order to introduce to the reader an entity we believe we are completely unrelated to. Paragraph 4 gives an example of an artificially constructed entity, a robot, which is dramatically contrasted with animals, because we perceive robots as emotionless beings. The difference between animals and robots is so extreme that the reader is persuaded to accept the thought that the real difference lies between animals and robots, not between animals and humans. By using Comparison & Contrast in such an effective fashion, Singer corrects the thought that animals are emotionless and incapable of feeling pain and persuades the reader to believe that animals do indeed feel pain.

Last but not least, Singer brings in evidence from accredited sources to back up his arguments. By citing Lord Brain, a very prominent figure, Singer adds credibility to his argument by showing that his arguments are supported by Lord Brain himself. This is especially important because up to this point all Singer's arguments have been based on his reasoning without any scientific evidence. The second piece of evidence Singer uses is an excerpt from a book about pain. Its main value does not come from the fact that this source is a book, but instead it plays a big role in summarizing Singer's arguments. "To Say that they feel less because they are less animals is an absurdity ⋯." This sort of quote-summary is very effective because it adds considerable weight to the author's argument.

NEW SAT ESSAY PREP SAT ESSAY PREP

READING 6

NEW SAT ESSAY PREP

Student DNA Polymerase
예비12, 2017 계관웅어학원 SAT advanced반

In their essay, Lindsey Shute and Benjamin Shute address the subject of farmlands and argue that government should make it easier for farmland to stay with farmers. In making their argument, the Shutes demonstrate logical reasoning based on comparison and contrast and utilize statistical evidence to firmly support their argument.

The authors' logical reasoning based on comparison and contrast could be seen in paragraph 3. They suppose that people would "think suitable land would be easy to find" due to the tax incentives in New York that "encourage nonfarmers to lent their land to farmers." The authors refute this notion by saying that "Most landlords offer only short-term leases" because "they don't want vegetable or livestock operations that bring traffic, workers, noise and fences." Then, the authors contrast this situatation with the necessity of "long-term land tenure for vegetable and livestock growers, who need years to build soil fertility, improve pasture and add infrastructure." Due to the landlords' preferances, the authors include that "only farms that grow low-value animal feed crops like hay, corn or beans are attracted to one year leases." Here the authors present two types of farms that either grew high-value corps or low value crops and demonstrate their contrasting natures in terms of agreement of land use with the landlords. By using the world "only" in front of the low-value-crops farm, readers could infer that high-value-crops farms are more important than their counterparts and that the preferences of nonfarmer landlords are basically preventing these farms to produce high-value crops. Thus his logical reasoning base on comparison and contrast is important, because it clearly shows that nonfarmers owning farming lands most likely prevents farmers from producing high-value crops.

Building on to this, the authors utilize statistical evidence and this could be seen in paragraphs 6, 8 and 9. In paragraph 6, the authors say that "in the next 20 years, 70 percent of the nation's farmland will change hands." They reveal that "most farm kids do not choose to carry on the family business." Despite this disadvantageous trend, the authors argue that for an "eager generation of younger farmers to farm, they need land and few will be able to secure it without help." In paragraph 8, the authors say that "eighty percent of farmers live in or near cities" and that "it's critical that farms ring those cities, and that farmers in the ring be protected." Lastly in paragraph 9, the authors refer to a recent study which "identified 614 vital unprotected farms in the Hudson Valley" and argue that New York City should invest in the protection of those farmlands to assure fresh food." All of these statistical evidence are followed by the authors' argument that farmlands should be protected. When the authors say protected, they include the notion of it being in the hands of farmers , evidenced in the statement "we want to pass our stewardship it this land on to future farmers." By revealing the magnitude and the seriousness of this issue through statistics, the authors could instil in the minds of the readers that farmlands should be protected by farmers. So theses statistical evidence are important, because they directly connect with and support the reasons why farmlands should stay with the farmers.

The Shutes demonstrate their logical reasoning based on comparison and contrast and utilize statistical evidence to support their claim. Without these rhetorical devices, the Shutes' argument wouldn't have been effective and powerful, as they intended it to be.

Problem 1:

Certain problems occur over and over again and are very difficult to get rid of. Here we have exactly the same problem we encountered in so many other essays: failing to identify one outstanding reasoning device: Cause & Effect. The other big problem is failing to identify Comparison & Contrast. Like evil spirits, these two problems haunt almost every essay I have ever dealt with.

Problem 2:

In the second paragraph student DNA Polymerase talks about the author, refuting something even before establishing what was compared and contrasted. This is a very bad style because it indicates that the writer of the essay is disorganized and that the essay itself is digressive.

Problem 3:

In the third paragraph this student discusses the Statistical Evidence put forth by the author, but simply mentioning this Statistical Evidence is not good enough, because the author effectively combined his or her reasoning device based on Comparison & Contrast, with Cause & Effect. It seems that student DNA Polymerase has not carefully analyzed the authors' overall rhetorical approaches.

+cause&effect

In their essay, Lindsey Shute and Benjamin Shute address the subject of farmlands and argue that government should make it easier for farmland to stay with farmers. In making their argument, the Shutes demonstrate logical reasoning based on comparison and contrast and utilize statistical evidence to firmly support their argument.

The authors' logical reasoning based on comparison and contrast could be seen in paragraph 3. They suppose that people would "think suitable land would be easy to find" due to the tax incentives in New York that "encourage non-farmers to lend their land to farmers." The authors refute this notion by saying that "most landlords offer only short-term leases" because "they don't want vegetable or livestock operations that bring traffic, workers, noise and fences." Then, the authors contrast this situation with the necessity of "long-term land tenure for vegetable and livestock growers, who need years to build soil fertility, improve pasture and add infrastructure." Due to the landlords' preferences, the authors include that "only farms that grow low-value animal feed crops like hay, corn or beans are attracted to one year leases." Here the authors present two types of farms that either grow high-value crops or low value crops and demonstrate their contrasting natures in terms of agreement of land use with the landlords. By using the world "only" infront of the low-value-crops farm, readers could infer that high-value-crops farms are more important than their counterparts and that the preferences of non farmer landlords are basically preventing these farms to produce high-value crops. Thus this logical reasoning based on comparison and contrast is important because it clearly shows that nonfarmers owning farming lands most likely prevents farmers from producing high-value crops.

Building on to this, the authors utilize statistical evidence and this could be seen in paragraphs 6, 8, and 9. In paragraph 6, the authors say that "in the next 20 years, 70 percent of the nation's farmland will change hands." They reveal that "most farm kids do not choose to carry on the family business." Despite this disadvantageous trend, the authors argue that for an "eager generation of younger farmers to farm, they need land and few will be able to secure it without help" In paragraph 8, the authors say that "eighty percent of farmers live in or near citits" and that "it's critical that farms ring those cities, and that farmers in the ring be protected." Lastly in paragraph 9, the authors refer to a recent study which "identified 614 vital unprotected forms in the Hudson Valley" and argues that New York City should invest in the protection of those farmlands to assure fresh food". All of these statistical evidence are followed by the authors' argument that farmlands should be protected. When the authors say protected, they include the notion of it being in the hands of farmers, evidenced in the statement "we want to pass our stewardship of this land on to future farmers." By revealing the magnitude and the seriousness of this issue through statistics, the authors could instil in the minds of the readers that farmlands should be protected by farmers. So these statistical evidence are important, because they directly connect with and support the reasons why farmlands should stay with the farmers.

Thus Shutes demonstrate their logical reasoning based on comparison and contrast and utilize statistical evidence to support their claim. Without these rhetorical devices, the Shutes' argument wouldn't have been effective and powerful, as they intended it to be.

Because you failed to identify one outstanding element half of your essay literally turned bland. 3.5/3/3.5 = 10X2 = 20/24

Sample Essay 22

Student Monarch Butterfly
예비12, 2017 계관웅어학원 SAT advanced반

In "Keep Farmland for Farmer," Lusher Shute and Benjamin Shute build on argument to persuade their audience that the government should help farmers to stay with farmland. The authors use reasoning such as comparison and contrast and utilize examples to support their argument.

The authors compare and contrast the short-term land and long-term land. Nonfarmers can rent their land to farmers by encouragement of tax incentives in New York. However, the authors say, "But long-term land tenure is essential for vegetable and livestock growers, ⋯ Only farms that grow low-value animal feed crops ⋯ are attracted to one-year leases." This does not seem to be truly beneficial for farmers who are motivated to farm. By comparing and contrasting the types of rental land, the authors can show the disadvantages of farmers to their audience because it shows the farmers' situation and concern.

The authors claim that the government needs to support farmers to preserve farmland. They says, "The United States Department of Agriculture spends money to preserve farms, but ⋯ there aren't enough." They use statistic example to support this claim. They state, "The need it well documented; a recent study identified 614 vital unprotected farms in the Hudson Valley … it need to do the same with farmland to assure fresh food." By showing the example, their audience may realize the government's protection is necessary because there are even many unprotected farms just in the Hudson Valley and they might think there are more farms should be protected.

Lusher Shute and Benjamin Shute clearly deliver their idea to their audience that the government should make it easier for farmland to stay with farmers. Their reasoning and example support their argument.

Problem 1:

Student Monarch Butterfly has again failed to identify one outstanding reasoning device: Cause & Effect. To make matters worse, the student failed to mention any personal examples used by the author and these examples serve a vital role in the author's argument.

Problem 2:

Other than Comparison & Contrast, this student failed to discuss, in significant detail, the author's other outstanding rhetorical devices and because of this oversight, the entire essay turned out rather simple and dull. Discussing other rhetorical devices would have allowed the student to realize and to demonstrate how effectively the author had combined them to convey the central idea.

Plus:

The discussion of the author's reasoning device based on Comparison & Contrast was well founded and to-the-point.

Not specific at all

In "Keep Farmland for Farmer," Lusher Shute and Benjamin Shute build an argument to persuade their audience that the ~~govery~~ government should help farmers to stay with farmland. The authors use reasoning such as comparison and contrast ✓ and utilize examples to support their argument.

+ personal example , → ~~comparison & contrast~~ + cause & effect

The authors compare and contrast the short-term land and long-term land. Nonfarmers can rent their land to farmers ✓ by encouragement of tax incentives in New York. However, the authors say, "But long-term land tenure is essential for vegetable and livestock growers, ⋯ Only farms that grow low-value animal feed crops ⋯ are attracted to one-year leases." This does not seem to be truly beneficial for farmers who are motivated to farm. By comparing and contrasting the types of rental land, the authors can show the disadvantages of farmers to their audience because it shows the farmers' situation and concern.

The authors claim that the government needs to support farmers to preserve farmland. They says, "The United States Department of Agriculture spends money to preserve farms, but ⋯ there aren't enough." They use statistic example to support this claim. They state, "The need is well documented: a recent study identified 614 vital unprotected farms in the Hudson Valley ⋯ it need to do the same with farmland to assure fresh food." By showing the example, their audience may realize the government's protection is neccessary because there are even many unprotected farms just in the Hudson Valley and they might think there are more farms should be protected.

Lusher Shute and Benjamin Shute clearly deliver their idea to their audience that the government should make it easier for farmland to stay with farmers. Their reasoning and example support their argument.

1. You missed 2 outstanding elements
   : personal example, cause & effect
2. Because of ①, you couldn't include
   an important analysis on the effective
   personal example, which is critical
   in ~~your~~ understanding the author's central idea

$$3/2/3 = 8 \times 2 = 16/24$$

Sample Essay 23

—

Student Parallelism
예비10, 2017 계관웅어학원 SAT advanced반

   In the passage, the authors Lindsey Lusher Shute and Benjamin Shute try to persuade their audience that the government should make it easier for farmland to stay with farmers. The authors use personal examples, statistic evidence and effective reasoning based on comparison and contrast to strengthen their argument.

   A personal example is used in the beginning of the passage. In paragraph one, the authors state that "When we went looking in upstate New York for a home for our farm, we feared competition from deep-pocketed developers. ⋯ Though the farms best suited for our vegetables were protected from developments, ⋯ we discovered that we couldn't compete, because conserved farmland is open to all buyers — millionaires included." Despite the subjective nature of the central idea, this example is effective in strengthening the central idea as it directly exposes the harsh conditions of the farmers, which will play a role in making the audience empathize with the authors' main argument and therefore turning to support it. The anecdote serves to set up the content that will follow, about how farmers do not have much chance against the rich who want farms for the "peace and quiet," not for agricultural purposes. It will also play as an effective introduction that can catch the readers' attention as it begins with a light but connotative story. The situation of most farmers is generalized in this part of the passage, within makes a connotative, but since it talks about the real experience of the authors, it is light as the same time, helping the readers stay engaged throughout the passage and to focus better on the central idea.

Additionally, in the ninth paragraph, the authors utilize statistical evidence and comparison and contrast to emphasize the need for New York City to "think about the land beyond the boroughs." "The need is well-documented: a recent study identified 614 vital unprotected farms in the Hudson Valley. New York City invested in the protection of its watershed in the Catskill; it needs to do the same with farmland to assure fresh food." The citing of a result of a related study adds power to the central idea as it has a subjective leaning. The numerical evidence solidifies the central idea. The comparison between Catskills and farmlands is also very effective; it clearly shows that although they are two equally different sectors, only Catskills gets the privilege to receive protection from New York City, not the farmland Why is it that only one sector of the food industry enjoys the protection of the city? The evident discrimination shown from this comparison and contrast can definitely play a part in urging for more support from the city. It strongly implies the importance of the authors' central idea.

The authors have utilized both personal and statistical evidence and strong reasoning to support their argument. Without these devices, the authors could not have succeeded in persuading as many readers.

Problem 1:

Student Parallelism failed to identify a reasoning device based on Cause & Effect, but fortunately did identify a personal example.

Problem 2:

In the third paragraph this student was smart enough to put Comparison & Contrast and Statistical Evidence together in the discussion, but for some reason stopped there. The student could have continued and discussed how effectively the authors combined the two in order to more effectively deliver their central idea.

Plus:

Student Parallelism not only identified and discussed the authors' personal example but also offered a reason why it was effective in conveying the central idea. Even if the reason offered did not make a lot of sense, simply mentioning it would probably be enough to get the student a higher score. Fortunately for this student and for you, ETS evaluators have only about 10-20 minutes to look at each individual essay.

Week 10-2 EW	NAME:	Class: Adv.

In the passage, the authors Lindsey Lusher Shute and Benjamin Shute try to persuade their audience that the government should make it easier for farmland to stay with farmers. The authors use personal examples, statistic evidence and effective reasoning based on comparison and contrast to strengthen their argument.

Surprisingly, this IS a very effective example, but you didn't explain why. (+ cause & effect)

A personal example is used in the beginning of the passage. In paragraph one, the authors state that "When we went looking in upstate New York for a home for our farm, we feared competition from deep-pocketed developers... Though the farms best suited for our vegetables were protected from developments,... we discovered that we couldn't compete, because conserved farmland is open to all buyers — millionaires included." Despite the subjective nature of the central idea, this example is effective in strengthening the central idea as it directly exposes the harsh conditions of the farmers, which will play a role in making the audience empathize with the authors' main argument, and therefore turning to support it. The anecdote serves to set up the content that will follow, about how farmers do not have much chance against the rich who want farms for the "peace and quiet", not for agricultural purposes. It will also play as an effective introduction that can catch the readers' attention as it begins with a light but connotative story. The situation of most farmers is generalized in this part of the passage, which makes a connotative, but since it talks about the real experience of the authors, it is light as the same time, helping the readers stay engaged throughout the passage and to focus better on the central idea.

Additionally, in the ninth paragraph, the authors utilize statistical evidence and comparison and contrast to emphasize the need for New York City to "think about the land beyond the boroughs." "The need is well-documented: a recent study identified 614 vital unprotected farms in the Hudson Valley. New York City invested in the protection of its watershed in the Catskills; it needs to do the same with farmland to assure fresh food." The citing of a result of a related study adds power to the central idea as it has a subjective leaning. The numerical evidence solidifies the central idea. The comparison between Catskills and farmlands is also very effective; it clearly shows that although they are two equally different sectors, only Catskills gets the privilege to receive protection from New York City, not the farmlands. (The evident discrimination shown from this comparison and contrast can definitely play a part in urging for more support from the city. Why is it that only one sector of the food industry enjoys the protection of the city? It strongly implies the importance of the authors' central idea.

   The authors have utilized both personal and statistical evidence and strong reasoning to support their argument. Without these devices, the authors could not have succeeded in persuading as many readers.

Student Meteorite
예비11, 2017 계관웅어학원 SAT advanced반

In "Keep Farmland for Farmers," Lusher Shute and Benjamin Shute build on argument to persuade their audience that the government should make it easier for farmland to stay with farmers. The authors offers personal evidence and use powerful reasoning such as cause & effect to strengthen the logic and persuasiveness of their argument.

In the beginning of the passage, the authors talk about their personal experience as being farmers. They say "when we went looking in upstate New York for a home for our farm, we feared competition from deep-pocketed developers, a new subdivision or a big-box store" and say "Though the farms best suited for our vegetables were protected from development by conservation easements, we discovered that we couldn't compete, because conserved farmland is open to all buyers—millionaires included." This explanation about the hardship and obstacles they have faced as a farmer effectively shows what is happening in the real farm life. Through the explanation, the audience will see the need of farmland conservation, because the farmers, who contribute to very big part of our life as providing essential foods, are the people who are now advocating for the further protection on their farmland. This type of personal evidence is very effective, because the normal people cannot easily imagine the reality of farm life, and thus the authors' personal evidence can give the audience a reasonable understanding of their central argument.

Lusher Shute and Benjamin Shute further strengthen their central argument by using powerful reasoning such as cause & effect. The causes, as authors says, are that "a non farmer had bought [the farmland]" and "most landlords offer only short-term leases," "but long-term land tenure is essential for vegetable and livestock growers, who need years to build soil fertility, improve posture and add infrastructure." Also the authors say that people, non-farmers, "added an air-conditioned home, a heated pool and asphalt drive" on their land, thus "the value increases so much that no working farmer can afford it." As on effect, they say "the Vermont Land Trust and the State of Massachusetts are keeping farmland in the hands of farmers through stricter conservation easements that limit who can own it, which keeps farms affordable and deters farm sales to nonfarmers." The authors can powerfully show the case of the government regulation is in effect as the solution for the problem, the lost of farmland. Now, the audience cannot deny the authors' arguments, since they saw the real case on which government put the regulation. Also the audience can fully understand what causes the problem and how can they solve it. This type of reasoning based on cause & effect is especially powerful because it further supports the authors' argument by showing the cause of the problem and the real adaptation of their suggestion in the same time.

By offering personal evidence and using powerful reasoning such as cause & effect, Lindsey Lusher Shute and Benjamin Shute could successfully persuade their audience to adopt their stance.

Problem 1:

The same nightmare revisited. Student Meteorite failed to identify one of the authors' outstanding devices: Comparison & Contrast. The student also failed to mention Statistical Evidence.

Problem 2:

Unfortunately, student Meteorite made some occasional grammatical errors, such as "in [at] the same time" at the end of the third paragraph and "as being farmers [as farmers]" at the beginning of the second paragraph.

Plus 1:

This student not only identified and thoroughly discussed the authors' personal example but also provided a reason why it was effective in conveying the author's central idea. In addition, the reason provided made a lot of sense. An ETS evaluator would surely notice this.

Plus 2:

Look at the discussion of Cause & Effect in the fourth paragraph. Student Meteorite knew exactly what to do; identify what caused what and demonstrate how effectively it was used. This made the student's essay appear organized and systematic. Student Meteorite employed a very practical and effective strategy in this perspective.

In "Keep Farmland for Farmers", Lusher Shute and Benjamin Shute build an argument to persuade their audience that the government should make it easier for farmland to stay with farmers. The authors offers personal evidence and use powerful reasoning such as cause & effect to strengthen the logic and persuasiveness of their argument. + comparison & contrast

In the beginning of the passage, the authors talk about their personal experience as being farmers. They say " When we went looking in upstate New York for a home for our farm, we feared competition from deep-pocketed developers, a new subdivision or a big-box store" and say " Though the farms best suited for our vegetables were protected from development by conservation easements, we discovered that we couldn't compete, because conserved farmland is open to all buyers - millionaires included." This explanation about the hardship and obstacles they have faced as a farmer effectively shows what is happening in the real farm life. Through this explanation, the audience will see the need of farmland conservation, because the farmers, who contribute to very big part of our life as providing essential foods, are the people who are now advocating for the further protection on their farmland. This type of personal evidence is very effective, because the normal people cannot easily imagine the reality of farm life, and thus the authors' personal evidence can give the audience a reasonable understanding of their central argument. very good.

Lusher Shute and Benjamin Shute further strengthen their central argument by using powerful reasoning such as cause & effect. The causes, as the authors say, are that " a non farmer had bought [the farm land]" and " most landlords offer only short-term leases" "but long-term land tenure is essential for vegetable and livestock growers, who need years to build soil fertility, improve pasture and add infrastructure." Also the authors say that people, non-farmers, "added an air-conditioned home, a heated pool and asphalt drive" on their land, thus "the value increases so much that no working farmer can afford it." As an effect, they say "the Vermont Land Trust and the state of Massachusetts are keeping farmland in the hands of farmers through stricter conservation easements that limit who can own it, which keeps farms affordable and deters farm sales to nonfarmers." The authors can powerfully show the case of the government regulation is in effect as

the solution for the problem; the lost of farmland. Now, the audience cannot deny the authors' argument, since they saw the real case on which government put the regulation. Also the audience can fully understand what causes the problem and how can they solve it. This type of reasoning based on cause&effect is especially powerful because it further supports the authors' argument by showing the cause and the real adaptation of their suggestion in the same time.
of the problem

By offering personal evidence and using powerful reasoning such as cause&effect, Lindsey Lusher Shute and Benjamin Shute could successfully persuade their audience to adopt their stance.

Even though you missed one very important element, the rest if your analysis did quite a good job

$$4 / 3 / 4 = 11 \times 2 = 22 / 24$$

NEW SAT ESSAY PREP

PREP

SAT

ESSAY

PREP

An Improved Version
of Sample Essay 24
for achieving the maximum score

In "Keep Farmland for Farmers," Lusher Shute and Benjamin Shute construct an argument that the government should make it easier for farmland to remain in use by farmers. To strengthen the logic and persuasiveness of their argument the authors offer personal evidence and use powerful reasoning devices such as that based on Cause & Effect as well as that based on Comparison & Contrast and statistical evidence

In the beginning of the passage, the authors talk about their personal experience as farmers. They say "when we went looking in upstate New York for a home for our farm, we feared competition from deep-pocketed developers, a new subdivision or a big-box store" and add "Though the farms best suited for our vegetables were protected from development by conservation easements, we discovered that we couldn't compete, because conserved farmland is open to all buyers — millionaires included." The authors' first-hand experience of the hardship and obstacles faced by farmers clearly illustrates what is happening in the real world. This is very effective because central ideas of this sort tend to be rather statistical and/or research-oriented. The explanation allows the reader to easily understand the need for farmland conservation; farmers make a big contribution to everyone's life by providing food, that indispensable element of everyday existence, and it is those same famers who are now advocating for further protection of their farmland. This type of personal evidence is especially effective partly because ordinary people cannot easily imagine the reality of farm life and the authors' personal experience can provide the reader with a better appreciation of their central argument.

The authors further strengthen their central argument by using a powerful reasoning device based on Cause & Effect. The causes, as authors argue, are that "a non-farmer had bought [the farmland]" and "most landlords offer only short-term leases," "but long-term land tenure is essential for vegetable and livestock growers, who need years to build soil fertility, improve pasture and add infrastructure." The authors also note that rural residents who are not farmers "added an air-conditioned home, a heated pool and asphalt drive" on their land, thus "the value increases so much that no working farmer can afford it." As to the effect, they say "the Vermont Land Trust and the State of Massachusetts are keeping farmland in the hands of farmers through stricter conservation easements that limit who can own it which keeps farms affordable and deters farm sales to nonfarmers." In this case the Cause & Effect strategy is quite effective because an argument based solely on personal experience might seem like nothing more than pathetic self interest. The authors argue effectively that in this case government regulation is the solution to the problem of the loss of farmland. The reader cannot easily deny the authors' arguments, since they are now aware of a real case in which government regulations were effectively applied. Also, the reader can fully understand what causes the problem and how that problem can be solved. This type of reasoning based on Cause & Effect is especially powerful because it further supports the authors' argument by making the authors' argument more specific and solidly grounded.

By citing personal experience and by using powerful reasoning device such as that of Cause & Effect, Lindsey Lusher Shute and Benjamin Shute could successfully persuade the reader that their point of view is the correct one.

Epilogue

One of the problems with manuals of this sort is that they have a very clear but narrow objective, which is to enable an average student to get the maximum score possible on a certain type of test. However, achieving this objective would require most students to spend an excessive amount of time upgrading their writing skills and this is just not practical. For that reason, this manual focuses on getting a *very good score* or the maximum score possible on the essay section of the SAT test. After getting into college, common sense dictates, that good students pay more attention to what is written in their textbooks and to what their professors say in lectures than what is written on the pages of this manual. Also, readers of this manual must never forget that the advice offered here has been written with the assumption that an ETS evaluator can only spend between 10 and 15 minutes reading and grading an individual essay.

Having pointed this out, it must also be noted that the strategies expressed in this manual are both practical and effective, and can be used for almost any type of rhetorical analysis. However just bear one thing in mind; this manual offers a solution to one specific problem; how can a student get a score between 22 and 24 on a specific test? Such strategies are not necessarily intended to be used for rhetorical analysis in other situations: "if you just try to explain how the author's particular rhetorical device is effective in conveying the central idea even if the explanation doesn't make much sense, you will get the perfect score." This solution works for a test like the SAT essay, and one of the reasons it works is that the evaluators simply do not have enough time to do a thorough job. However, writing a paper in university is of a completely different nature. When writing a paper that will be read and evaluated by a university professor, your explanation must make good sense based on the reading assignment. A student, who keeps this in mind and applies these strategies with caution, will find this manual a very valuable asset.

이 책에 에세이 수록을 허락해 주신 학생 여러분과
감수를 맡아주신 원어민 선생님께 감사드립니다.

원어민 감수 | Robert Allan Webster
- 캐나다 빅토리아 대학교 언어학과 졸업
- 한국 유수의 학원에서 28년간 강의

New SAT Essay Prep

24 Actual Sample Essays with
Detailed and Logical Problem Analyses

초판 1쇄 인쇄 2018년 1월 5일
초판 1쇄 발행 2018년 1월 10일

지은이 **계관웅**
발행처 **사냥꾼**
발행인 **계관웅**
표지 디자인 **이정훈**
본문 디자인 **보임디자인(주)**
전산 **최원석**

출판신고 등록번호 **제2006-000210호**
주소 **서울시 강남구 삼성로 324, 3층(대치동, 신해청상가)**
전화 **02-554-9897**
팩스 **02-553-9895**
이메일 **xpertprep@naver.com**

값 23,000원

ISBN 979-11-954910-4-9